AUSTRALIA AND NEW ZEALAND
The Law Book Company Ltd.
Sydney : Melbourne : Perth

CANADA AND U.S.A.
The Carswell Company Ltd.
Agincourt, Ontario

INDIA
N.M. Tripathi Private Ltd.
Bombay
and
Eastern Law House Private Ltd.
Calcutta and Delhi
M.P.P. House
Bangalore

ISRAEL
Steimatzky's Agency Ltd.
Jerusalem : Tel Aviv : Haifa

PAKISTAN
Pakistan Law House
Karachi

CONSTITUTIONAL FUNDAMENTALS

by
SIR WILLIAM WADE
Q.C., LL.D., F.B.A.
Formerly Master of Gonville and Caius College, Cambridge

Revised edition

Published under the auspices of
THE HAMLYN TRUST

LONDON
STEVENS & SONS
1989

Published in 1989 by
Stevens & Sons Limited of
South Quay Plaza
183 Marsh Wall, London E14 9FT

Laserset by
LBJ Enterprises Limited
Chilcompton, Somerset

Printed in Scotland

Second Impression 1983
Third Impression 1986
Revised Edition 1989

British Library Cataloguing in Publication Data

Wade, H. W. R. (Henry William Rawson), *1918–*
   Constitutional fundamentals. — Rev. ed.
   1. Great Britain. Constitutional law
   I. Title
   344.102

   ISBN 0–420–47830–2 ✓
      0165379

CONTENTS

THE HAMLYN LECTURES

THE HAMLYN TRUST

THE Hamlyn Trust came into existence under the will of the late Miss Emma Warburton Hamlyn, of Torquay, who died in 1941 at the age of eighty. She came of an old and well-known Devon family. Her father, William Bussell Hamlyn, practised in Torquay as a solicitor for many years. She was a woman of strong character, intelligent and cultured, well versed in literature, music and art, and a lover of her country. She inherited a taste for law, and studied the subject. She also travelled frequently on the Continent and about the Mediterranean, and gathered impressions of comparative jurisprudence and ethnology.

Miss Hamlyn bequeathed the residue of her estate in terms which were thought vague. The matter was taken to the Chancery Division of the High Court, which on November 29, 1948, approved a Scheme for the administration of the Trust. Paragraph 3 of the Scheme is as follows:

> "The object of the charity is the furtherance by lectures or otherwise among the Common People of the United Kingdom of Great Britain and Northern Ireland of the knowledge of the Comparative Jurisprudence and the Ethnology of the chief European countries including the United Kingdom, and the circumstances of the growth of such jurisprudence to the intent that the Common People of the United Kingdom may realise the privileges which in law and custom they enjoy in comparison with other European Peoples and realising and appreciating such privileges may recognise the responsibilities and obligations attaching to them."

From the first the Trustees decided to organise courses of lectures of outstanding interest and quality by persons of eminence, under the auspices of co-operating Universities or other bodies, with a view to the lectures being made available in book form to a wide public.

The Thirty-Second Series of Hamlyn Lectures was delivered in May 1980 by Professor H. W. R. Wade in London.

A. L. DIAMOND,
Chairman of the Trustees.

May 1980

I am much indebted to my friend and colleague Mr. D. G. T. Williams, who kindly read these lectures both in draft and in proof and gave me valuable comments.

H.W.R.W.

December 18, 1979

These lectures, as now republished, are better described as a revised than as a second edition. On the whole it has seemed best to leave them in the form in which they were delivered, though I have made a few small changes where anachronistic time references, such as "last year," might jar upon the reader. Footnotes have been added to deal with later developments and these are indicated by the letters added to their clues (*e.g.* 10a). Some of the original footnotes have been expanded for the same purpose.

H.W.R.W.

June 19, 1989

TABLE OF CASES

TABLE OF STATUTES

Chapter 1

THE UNREFORMED CONSTITUTION

It is with an uneasy conscience that I deliver these lectures under the aegis of the Hamlyn Trust. For I ought, I know, to be exhorting the common people of the United Kingdom, as they are called by the Trust, to rejoice in the blessings which their laws and customs bestow upon them. But I am going to speak about the constitution, and the apportionment and exercise of power under it, and these are not matters about which I can invite the common people, whoever they may be, to feel unqualified satisfaction. But the Trustees were so kind as to approve my plan and I am comforted to think that if the Attorney-General should bring proceedings for breach of a public trust, it is they and not I whom he should call to account. If only I had the viewpoint of a Blackstone, a Bagehot or a Dicey, I could make my lectures glow with admiration of our institutions and of our national genius for adapting what is ancient and obsolete to new and beneficial purposes. To those famous names I should add that of Lord Denning, whose celebrated lectures, the first of the Hamlyn series, gave due praise to the great British achievement of freedom under law. I must myself hope, to adapt a well known judicial bon mot, that when my time comes to cross the Styx I will not see Miss Hamlyn's shade waiting for me reproachfully on the other side.

My plan is to examine various features of the constitution under four heads: Representation; Legislation; Administration; and Adjudication. I shall wander outside the familiar paths explored by books on constitutional law, which are for the most part content to describe in dispassionate detail institutions whose merits may be highly debatable. Perhaps in this respect the attitude of constitutional lawyers is in a transitional phase. The Blackstone-Bagehot-Dicey era was the age of self-satisfaction. Their successors today adopt a stance of fairly strict neutrality. The next era, I hope, will be that of the critics. Their service will be to hammer home the need for constitutional reform. The danger before them is obvious: this path leads straight into politics. But if the price of preserving the purity of constitutional law is that one must ignore the political pros and cons of what are, after all, our most essential laws, then I would say that the price is too high and the lack of realism is excessive. This is the world in which political scientists and economists have to live in any case. Why should it not be habitable by lawyers?

I need to spend little time in pointing out that there is now deep dissatisfaction with the constitution. Hardly a week passes without some new call for a Bill of Rights, entrenched clauses, a parliamentary committee system, fixed term parliaments, proportional representation, reform (or abolition) of the House of Lords, or some other radical change. Not long ago Lord Rawlinson drew attention to the fact that Parliament had commissioned inquiries and passed legislation on almost every aspect of life but that the one subject that seemed to be sacrosanct was Parliament itself. He proposed a full scale constitutional conference to include the electoral system, the role of Parliament, the method of legislation and the effects of the party system. The Royal Commission on the Constitution of 1969–1973 had terms of reference which could—and should, according to a minority of its members—have been wide enough for a grand inquest of this kind, but the majority considered themselves confined to the issue of devolution. Yet, as the majority themselves observed, there has never been any general review of the constitution as a whole, although the functions and the nature of government and the operation of the party system have changed beyond the dreams of earlier generations whose problems and practices gave rise to our constitutional laws and conventions.

The one specific procedure which exists for the purposes of constitutional reform is the Speaker's Conference[1]—though if it just deserves to be called a procedure, it may scarcely deserve to be called specific. It is really no more than an ad hoc committee of Members of Parliament selected by the Speaker from the principal parties, which is commissioned from time to time to discuss questions of electoral reform and to make recommendations. This has happened five times, all in the present century: 1916, 1929, 1944, 1965 and 1973. It might have happened again in 1974 had the Liberal party leader accepted Mr. Heath's offer of a Speaker's Conference on proportional representation. A Speaker's Conference usually has about 30 members with the Speaker in the chair. It has no legislative status or powers of any kind. It is not even given its terms of reference by Parliament: they are given by the government, after discussion with party leaders, and are set out in a letter from the Prime Minister inviting the Speaker to select the members and to preside. But in fact there are no firm rules. The Conference of 1929 was given no terms of reference, but decided to concern itself with proportional representation and the alternative vote, of which more hereafter. The terms of reference of the Conferences of 1965 and 1973 were not even debated in Parliament. Furthermore, Speaker's Conferences sit in private and publish no reasons for their recommendations. Admittedly they have paved the way for some important reforms, such as votes for women in 1918, as well as for many less important ones. Sir Winston Churchill claimed in 1948 that constitutional changes

---

[1] See E. Lyon and A. Wigram, *The Speaker's Conference* (Conservative Action for Electoral Reform, 1977).

should be made by agreement of party leaders or by conference under the impartial guidance of Mr. Speaker. But this optimistic proposition is honoured as much in the breach as in the observance. Governments have made many constitutional changes without inter-party agreement, and not merely without the recommendations of a Speaker's Conference but in direct contradiction of them—as with the abolition of the City of London franchise and the university franchise in 1948. At its best, the Speaker's Conference is a frail advisory mechanism, at the mercy of the government of the day. It is altogether useless when the question is one like proportional representation, the agitation of which the leaders of both the major parties wish to prevent at all costs. They are the sitting tenants of the political system, they are content with the monopoly of power that it gives them, and in this situation the prospects of reform from within Parliament are small indeed.

One's thoughts then turn wistfully to schemes of initiative and referendum as used in North America, particularly since the spectacular instance in 1978 when the voters of California rose in rebellion against over-taxation and forced a referendum which overrode the policies of government and legislature. This is a logical democratic safety-valve against governments which ignore the popular will but it would be visionary to hope for it in this country. We can only trust that in time there will be such a build-up of public opinion in favour of a thorough constitutional overhaul that one or both of the great parties will see that there is an electoral harvest to be reaped. Meanwhile I am glad that impetus has come from eminent lawyers such as Lord Scarman, Lord Hailsham and Professor Hood Phillips.

Chapter 2

REPRESENTATION

INEQUALITY OF CONSTITUENCIES

The first and foremost object of reforming zeal ought in my opinion to be the system of Parliamentary representation, or rather misrepresentation.

Let us first look at the distribution of constituencies. The English, Welsh, Scottish and Northern Irish constituencies are kept under separate review by the four Boundary Commissions, and normally (except in 1969 when the government procured their rejection by Parliament) their recommendations are duly approved by both Houses. They are, however, bound by the statutory allocation of seats to the three smaller territories, since it is decreed by statute that Scotland shall have not less than 71 seats, Wales not less than 35 and Northern Ireland 17.[1] Great Britain as a whole is to have a number "not substantially greater or less than 613." The number is now 618.

The effect of these quotas is, according to the Kilbrandon Report,[2] that Scotland is over-represented to the extent of 14 seats and Wales to the extent of five seats. Northern Ireland's recently-augmented quota of 17 seats is now correct. This is on the basis of constituencies of equal average population throughout the United Kingdom. The Scottish and Welsh over-representation is aggravated by the fact that on the same basis of calculation England should have 14 more seats (525 instead of 511). The only justification ever given for these ine-

[1] House of Commons (Redistribution of Seats) Acts 1949, 1979.
[2] Report of the Royal Commission on the Constitution, Cmnd. 5460 (1973), paras. 100 (note), 814.

qualities is that constituencies in sparsely populated areas such as the Highlands would otherwise be inconveniently large geographically.[3] But why should a thinly-spread population be entitled to more representation than it proportionately deserves? Why should it be supposed that those who dwell in the remoter parts of the country can vote less easily than others and so need a political weighting in their favour? Some idea of this kind must be rooted in psephological theory, since it appears in the rules under which the Boundary Commission are required to work in the four different countries. They may depart from the strict application of the electoral quota system if they think this is desirable on account of "special geographical considerations, including in particular the size, shape and accessibility of a constituency."[4] Just how these factors justify weighting one citizen's vote against another's is not explained and I do not profess to understand the implications. Even if it should be a legitimate argument in respect of sparse constituencies, which I doubt, I do not see how it can apply to a whole country such as Scotland or Wales. It seems plain that the English voter is not being given a fair deal, and all the more so now that Northern Ireland's under-representation is to be remedied by increasing her seats to 17 under the House of Commons (Redistribution of Seats) Act 1979.[4a]

Yet the under-representation of remote or sparsely populated areas seems to be a feature of many electoral systems. When Sir Ivor Jennings was helping to frame the independence constitution of Ceylon he said that the politicians called it "giving votes to the elephants and

---

[3] But even by this criterion the over-representation is excessive: see *Adversary Politics and Electoral Reform* (Finer ed.), p. 65.
[4] House of Commons (Redistribution of Seats) Act 1949, Sched. 2, r. 6.
[4a] Since replaced by the Parliamentary Constituencies Act 1986. For details concerning the "Celtic preference," see [1987] Pub. L. 324 (H. F. Rawlings).

the fishes."[5] In the case of Scotland it might be called giving votes to the deer and the salmon. I do not think that the deer and the salmon can complain that they have not been generously treated. Scotland's 14 additional seats are a very substantial political subsidy, especially in the periods of small government majorities, which occur quite frequently. Even the excess of five seats enjoyed by Wales may be enough to determine the fate of governments. If Celtic sympathy should cause Scotland and Wales to vote together against England, their surplus of 19 combined with the English deficiency of 14 gives them an advantage of 33 seats. When devolution was proposed for Scotland in 1978 Scotland's share of the seats at Westminster should have been proportionately less instead of proportionately more. England was to be deprived of any share in a great deal of Scottish legislation, yet Scotland was to retain not only a share in all English legislation but a share which, in proportion to population, was substantially more than the English share. The Kilbrandon Report observed that this might be argued to be undemocratic and a grave injustice to the people of England, and that there would be much to be said for reducing the Scottish and Welsh representation in terms of population to a lower level than the English, as in the case of Northern Ireland.[6] The Blake Commission, in its Report of 1976 for the Hansard Society, did not consider that devolution by itself justified under-representation at Westminster but equally it opposed over-representation.[7] Yet the only adjustment made by Parliament in the devolution legislation, and that only a minor palliative, was the House of Lords' successful amendment to the effect that Bills affecting England

[5] Jennings, "The Making of a Dominion Constitution" (1949) 65 L.Q.R. 456, 460.
[6] para. 815.
[7] Commission on Electoral Reform (Hansard Society, 1976), para. 44.

only, if carried by the aid of Scottish votes, should be reconsidered after an interval.[8] The situation would have been fundamentally unfair, and the House of Commons when passing the devolution legislation deliberately refrained from redressing it.

Within the constituent countries of the United Kingdom there are great inequalities in the size of individual constituencies. These are in principle less objectionable, in that they do not favour any one region of the country, and also in that there is standing machinery for correcting them through the Boundary Commission's reviews. But when the smallest constituency contains only 25,000 voters and the largest 96,000—nearly four times as many—it is hard to see how such uneven weighting of votes can be justified. The Blake Commission recommended that the discrepancy should never exceed two to one, except in the Scottish island areas,[9] and this is surely the maximum which should be regarded as tolerable. In the United States, where Congress showed similar unwillingness to rectify electoral injustice, in that case the over-representation of rural areas which resulted from the shift of population to the cities, the Supreme Court came to the rescue in its famous decision in *Baker* v. *Carr* (1962),[10] holding that failure by the State of Tennessee to provide constituencies on a broad basis of equality of population was a breach of the Fourteenth Amendment's guarantee of "the equal protection of the laws." In a similar case of 1964 concerning Alabama Chief Justice Warren said: "Legislators represent people, not trees or acres. Legislators are elected by voters, not farms or cities or economic interests . . . the basic principle of representative government remains, and must remain, unchanged—the weight of a citizen's vote

[8] Scotland Act 1978, s.66.
[9] para. 45.
[10] 369 U.S. 186 (1962).

cannot be made to depend on where he lives."[11] This, the Supreme Court said, was one of the fundamentals of democratic government. The British Parliament, addicted though it is to the pursuit of equality in so many other ways, does not seem interested in equality of representation between voters any more than between the different parts of the United Kingdom. Since 1948 it has insisted rigidly on the principle of one man, one vote. When will it accept the correlative principle of one vote, one value?

The blow struck by the Supreme Court of the United States vividly illustrates the benefits to be derived from fundamental constitutional rights established by law. The fact that it was a naked piece of judicial legislation, and that "the equal protection of the laws" had not previously been supposed to have anything to do with electoral equality, in no way detracts from the achievement. It is part of the function of a constitutional court to extend the protection of the law to rights which come to be recognised as fundamental, and countries whose constitutions provide for this give a fairer deal to their citizens than those which leave all such matters to politicians. In Britain we are so short of constitutional rights and our notion of the judicial function is so restricted, that electoral fairness is hardly thought to be the concern of lawyers. In the United States, on the other hand, it can be enforced as one of the legal essentials of democracy.

MISREPRESENTATION OF THE ELECTORATE

Even more fundamental questions arise when we turn to the relation between seats and votes and the absurdities

---

[11] *Reynolds* v. *Sims* 377 U.S. 533, 562 (1964). These decisions have not been followed in Australia: *Att.-Gen. for Australia* v. *Commonwealth* (1975) 135 C.L.R. 1.

produced by what is called the "first past the post" system of election. I do not know who invented that soubriquet; it is singularly inept and I decline to adopt it. It suggests that there is a winning post at some fixed point, *i.e.* some quota of votes, which the candidates can reach in succession. This is exactly what is not true of the existing system, but it is true of proportional representation by the single transferable vote. Psephologists, I believe, prefer to speak of the "relative majority" system. Personally I would call it the crude majority system, but in order not to be accused of tendentious nomenclature I shall call it the simple majority system, which seems to me to do it justice without inaccuracy, particularly since simplicity is about its only virtue. The same title was used by the White Paper of 1977 on Direct Elections to the European Assembly.[12]

If it is accepted that a democratic parliament ought to represent so far as possible the preference of the voters, this system is probably the worst that could be devised. This is now so well known that I need spend little time belabouring it. In particular, it is generally understood how it gives grossly exaggerated representation to the two major parties and is extremely unfair to smaller parties. The injustice to the Liberals at the two elections of 1974 is of course notorious: in the February election they polled over six million votes, more than half the winning Labour vote, yet received only 14 seats to Labour's 301. In the October election their share of the vote at 5.3 million was over half that of the Conservatives at 10.4 million, yet they obtained 13 seats and the Conservatives 277. But dozens of equally capricious results could be instanced. The general elections of 1950 and 1951 are characteristic examples. In that of 1950 the Labour government, which had been in office for four and a half years after its landslide victory of 1945, was

[12] Cmnd. 6768 (1977).

returned to power with 315 seats and a tiny overall majority of five. But it actually increased its vote by well over a million. The crushing victory of 1945 gave it 393 seats for 12 million votes. The marginal victory of 1950 gave it 315 seats for 13.3 million votes, so that one and a quarter million more votes produced 78 fewer seats. In terms of seats, the new Parliament seemed to show that the voters were disenchanted with Labour and nearly ready for a change. In terms of votes, it was a substantial victory. Then in 1951 Labour again increased its vote, attaining its highest-ever percentage of the poll and polling more votes than the Conservatives, yet the Conservatives were the winners with 26 more seats than Labour. In February 1974, on the other hand, it was Labour's turn to win a majority of seats on a minority of votes, though the margins in both cases were small. So it is not only small parties which are unfairly treated by the system; as between the two main parties it turns winners into losers and losers into winners. This is the result of paying attention only to who comes top of the poll in each constituency and of paying none to the size of the majority. Vast numbers of votes are simply disregarded and the preferences expressed are given no effect whatever.

MODERATION OR EXTREMISM?

The Blake Commission and other advocates of a fairer electoral system have many trenchant comments to make on this state of affairs. They point out that, though both the major parties doggedly support it, even they make no attempt to justify it as fair. They justify it by saying that in practice it works well since it produces effective majorities and strong governments, whereas proportional systems, they say, produce a multiplicity of parties and weak coalition governments. The arbitrary results are the price that has to be paid for the clear-cut two-party system which has always been the basis of British politics. The two-party system, in its turn, is supposed to have the virtue of a tendency towards moderation. Both the right and the left, it is argued, will take little account of their extremists, whose votes can be counted upon in any case, and will woo the floating voter in the middle. Thus the two-party system is said to generate a centripetal political force which keeps the country on a steady middle course and works against extremism. It is designed to produce what Bagehot called "the precise species of moderation most agreeable to the nation at large."

But in the light of present day reality this description sounds like a parody. It is a commonplace now to bewail the polarisation of party politics, the instability which it has brought upon the country, and the tendency towards extremism. The supposed centripetal force has become a centrifugal force. This is particularly striking in comparison with our European neighbours, for example France and West Germany, which have enjoyed much greater stability ever since the war, with an absence of violent swings from one political pole to another and with more consistency and moderation. In Britain we have two dominant parties with radically opposed political philosophies and an electoral system which ensures that they change places every few years, though not necessarily in accordance with the majority of votes. We are all familiar with the sharp reversals of policy which have been so unsettling and destructive. Nationalisation, education, housing, industrial relations, investment grants, taxation, pensions, incomes policy, expropriation—it is hardly possible to name an important sphere of domestic policy which has not been made a political football. Legislation, instead of contributing to steady progress and reform, comes to be regarded as a form of partisan warfare, to be forced through whenever the parliamentary situation permits and to be repealed at the next turn of the wheel in the electorate lottery. Powerful groups have been tempted to disobey Acts of Parliament, knowing that their political friends would secure their repeal when next returned to power. This is not a party matter. We have seen one party doing it to resist the reorganisation of schools and another doing it in industrial relations. Thus both the law and the constitution are brought into contempt.

It is plain that these tendencies, so far from favouring moderation and the middle way, favour just the opposite. We saw not so long ago how in the period before a general election the voices of the extremists of both parties suddenly became muted. It is in their interests not to frighten the voters, but to rely on the arbitrary results of the voting under which they have a good chance of an undue share of power. We have also seen, as the Blake Commission observed, a decline in the support for the two major parties combined with the increase of polarisation between them. In the 1950s Labour and Conservatives between them took some 97 per cent. of the total vote, whereas by 1974 their combined share had sunk to 75 per cent. "What does seem clear," the Commission say, "is that over the last 10 years (to 1977) the gap has increased, is increasing and shows no sign of being diminished. The situation is exacerbated by the promulgation of highly detailed manifestos designed to placate every faction within a party but seldom read, let alone endorsed, by the bulk of its supporters. If the government which they elect feels—or claims to feel—obliged to implement the manifesto in every detail, Britain might find herself governed by a minority within a minority."[13] Thus there is an ever-present danger of our electoral system producing what the Commission call "flagrant minority rule." "It

[13] para. 38.

does not prevent governments from pursuing policies which are manifestly against the will of the majority."[14] And the greater the polarisation between the parties, the more serious is the danger.

That this polarisation is aggravated by the electoral system is equally clear to other expert commentators. As Professor Finer explains, by its unfairness to small parties the system produces a rigid two-party confrontation in Parliament and "puts a formidable premium upon party solidarity."[15]; He then demonstrates both textually and diagramatically how this gives undue influence to extremists on both sides. On any given issue each party's point of compromise will be near the mid-point of its own spectrum, *i.e.* far to the right or the left of the true mid-point of Parliamentary opinion as a whole. The true centre, that is the left wing of the right combined with the right wing of the left, is never mobilised at all. Yet this central body of opinion probably corresponds best to the wishes of the electorate as a whole. It is because the extremists pull each party's point of compromise well to the right or well to the left of centre that we get the succession of reversal policies which, as any one can see, have been so damaging. The system is calculated to produce the maximum antagonism and instability and the minimum consensus and consistency.

This must be as serious a defect as it is possible for a democratic constitution to have. There can be no doubt that it is being exploited, and there is no doubt in my own mind that it has much to do with the misgovernment from which Britain has suffered. I cannot help quoting, since it reveals the situation so candidly, the guidance issued several times in 1976 and 1977 by the General Secretary of the Labour Party, urging that Labour supporters should oppose proportional representation as the method of election for the European Parliament. His

[14] para. 42.
[15] *Adversary Politics and Electoral Reform*, pp. 9, 12–13.

argument was that it would then become difficult to resist pressure for proportional representation in the British Parliament and he was reported as saying: "Proportional representation means coalition government at Westminster on the lines of our European partners, and it is goodby then to any dreams or aspirations for a democratic socialist Britain." There could hardly be a more honest admission that the party could not carry out its policy if the voting system fairly reflected the wishes of the electors and that it must rely on the possibilities, indeed probabilities, of what the Blake Commission called "flagrant minority rule." You will have noticed that it is a "democratic" Britain that is to be attained by these means. But to force a policy through Parliament when it is known that the majority of voters are opposed to it is not every one's idea of democracy.

It is only through the spectacles of hardened party politicians that coalition government can be seen as undemocratic or objectionable, at any rate at times when the electorate is deeply divided and evenly balanced between the two main parties, and when voters are deserting the main parties in favour of third parties. This was happening in both the elections of 1974, when the Liberals polled about twice as many votes as they had attained in any election since the war, showing that voters were becoming disenchanted with the state of two-party politics. Yet almost all these significant votes were wasted. I suspect that too much reverence has been paid to Disraeli's dictum that England does not love coalitions, and that this doctrine is more favoured by professional politicians than it is by those who are governed by them. There are times when coalitions are suitable and times when they are unsuitable, but when opinion in the country is in a state of equilibrium a coalition may well be a more democratic solution than the solution produced by the crude and antagonistic system which we have now. A coalition gives each party a share in the government and favours the centrist policies and moderation instead of extremism followed by reversal. It may well be better than the "elective dictatorship," as Lord Hailsham calls it, when one party monopolises the immense power and patronage which its domination over Parliament gives it.

Nor is it true that coalition governments are necessarily weak. Professor Finer and his colleagues have scotched that allegation too.[16] Nor is there any evident merit in the other conventional objections. The Blake Commission discounted the argument that the possibility of coalitions meant giving too much power to minority parties "in backstage bargains and wheeler-dealing in smoke-filled rooms."[17] This may occur in any system, as we saw in February 1974. Where the majority of voters supported one party the Commission felt that single party government was preferable and that the ideal electoral system should contain a slight but not a strong bias in favour of it. This is very far from a condemnation of coalitions as such.

When all else fails, upholders of the present simple majority system fall back on the "strong government" argument. But this argument is double-edged. Strong government is a positive evil if it operates contrary to the opinion of the majority. Furthermore, the stronger government is the more damage is likely to be done by swinging from one extreme to another at times when there is a high degree of polarisation between the two main parties. The forces of moderation as well as those of activism need to be fairly represented. The "strong government" argument is merely another way of saying that an electoral system which yields capricious results is likely to give a working majority to one party or the other by denying fair representation to minorities who

[16] *Ibid.* pp. 26, 82, 306.
[17] para. 62.

might otherwise hold the balance of power. As a constitutional principle this seems to me to contain more vice than virtue.

PROJECTS OF REFORM

The case for electoral reform, which now seems so strong, was in fact taken much more seriously in the first half of this century than it has hitherto been in the second. A Royal Commission on Electoral Systems was appointed in 1900 and reported in 1910 in favour of changing to the system known as the alternative vote. Parliament took no action until 1918, by which time opinion had progressed still further towards proportional representation. The Representation of the People Act 1918, which followed a Speaker's Conference, took two steps towards proportional representation by single transferable vote: first it introduced this system for the university constituencies (which had existed since 1603); and secondly it provided for a Royal Commission to prepare a scheme for its use in 100 seats in the House of Commons, to take effect if approved by resolutions of both Houses. But when the scheme came before them, and was approved by the Lords, the Commons decided that they preferred the alternative vote. So nothing was done, and the old system which neither House then wished to employ was kept in being merely because the Houses could not agree on how to replace it. Another effort was made in 1929–1930, when a Speaker's Conference obtained evidence of the systems used in foreign countries and voted by a majority for proportional representation. But since the vote was on party lines (Conservatives and Liberals in favour, Labour against) there was no formal recommendation. Then in 1931 the Labour government, under Liberal pressure, brought in a Bill providing for adoption of the alternative vote system, but this was lost when the government fell in the same year. Meanwhile proportional representation by the single transferable vote had been in use in Northern Ireland from 1920 to 1929, when it was abolished, probably in an evil hour, by the Northern Ireland Parliament. That is the sorry tale of the abortive attempts at reform. Party opinion subsequently hardened against it, and it was rejected out of hand by the Speaker's Conferences of 1944 and 1965. Even the one small achievement of proportional representation in the university seats was removed in 1948 when the university vote was abolished, contrary to the Speaker's Conference recommendation. The Speaker's Conference of 1973 did not even consider the subject.

There are now many signs of a revival of public interest. In addition to the obvious causes—the conspicuous failure to produce representative and moderate government and the disenchantment with the two-party option—there has been the stimulus given by the schemes for the Scottish and Welsh Assemblies, abortive though they proved; by the direct elections to the European Parliament; by the ill-fated "power-sharing" experiments in Northern Ireland, in which simple majority voting would plainly have been intolerable; and by Northern Irish local government elections. The Kilbrandon Report recommended that the regional assemblies should be elected by the system of single transferable vote and on Lord Kilbrandon's own motion an amendment in favour of the additional member system was carried by a large majority (including members of all parties) in the course of the passage of the Scotland Act 1978. But the House of Commons rejected it, as they also rejected all proposals for proportional systems in the elections to the European Parliament. In the latter case the government did at least publish a White Paper explaining various proportional systems, but warning darkly that to adopt any of them "would be a major constitutional innovation, the consequences of which are difficult to foresee.''[18] In fact one consequence is easy to foresee: much fairer and more democratic results. The Treaty of Rome provides that ultimately there shall be a uniform procedure for elections to the European Parliament, to be drawn up by that Parliament itself.[19] Since all the other EEC countries except France[19a] use proportional representation, it seems highly unlikely that the crude British system will be adopted in the end and highly likely that in this sphere at least a fairer system will prove irresistible. Meanwhile there is growing support for domestic electoral reform. In May 1978 a poll carried out by the Opinion Research Centre showed a 68 per cent. vote for proportional representation in Britain and an 82 per cent. vote for letting the question be decided by a referendum rather than by Parliament. This latter figure emphasises once again the gulf between Parliament and public opinion which voters feel to exist. Even so, there is a select band of reformist M.P.s of all parties who have consistently voted for proportional representation in the devolution and European election debates. But so long as the leaders of the two great parties agree on rejecting all change, the outlook must remain depressing.

PROPORTIONAL VOTING SYSTEMS

I cannot on this occasion describe in much detail the various preferential and proportional voting systems from which a choice will have to be made if, as I hope, we reach the point of reform.[20] Scores of different

---

[18] Cmnd. 6768 (1977), para. 17.
[19] Article 138.3.
[19a] France used proportional systems in 1945–1958 and 1985–1986, but after each period replaced P.R. with the two-round majority system.
[20] For a brief conspectus, see *An ABC of Electoral Systems* (Parliamentary Democracy Trust, 1978).

systems have been advocated at different times, but at present there are four around which discussion revolves. First there is the alternative vote, which was recommended by the Royal Commission of 1910. This system is preferential but not proportional. The voter may list the candidates in his constituency in his order of preference, and if no one candidate has an absolute majority of first preferences the lowest-scoring candidate is eliminated and his second preferences are distributed among the others, the process being repeated if necessary until a clear majority is produced. This system solves the problem of splitting the vote and of winning on a minority vote. It helps small parties by eliminating the feeling that votes for them are wasted, but it does not otherwise help them to obtain a share of seats proportional to their total vote. Akin to this is the double ballot, as now used in France, which allows electors to reconsider their votes a few days later if the first ballot shows that they would be wasted.

Of the genuinely proportional systems the most straightforward is that of the party list. In its simplest form the parties publish their lists of candidates and the electors must vote for one or other list as a whole, the seats then being allotted in proportion to the aggregate vote of each party. But of course that removes the personal connection between constituent and member, and no European country uses it in so rudimentary a form. It is in combination with devices enabling the voter to indicate his preference among the listed candidates that the list system is popular, and various such combinations are in use in the Benelux countries, Sweden, Switzerland, Denmark and Italy, with multi-member constituencies.[21] West Germany has another variant

---

[21] See E. Lakeman, *How Democracies Vote* (4th ed., 1974); *Nine Democracies* (electoral systems of the countries then in the EEC, 1978); *Power to Elect* (1982).

which the Blake Commission considered to be the best model for Britain, though subject to modifications. This is a mixture of single-member constituencies with additional members added in such a way as to bring the strength of the parties into proportion with their aggregate vote. So it is called the "additional member" system.[22] In West Germany half the seats are directly elected and the other half are filled from the party lists on a regional basis, each voter having two votes, one for a candidate and one for a party. The Blake Commission preferred a single-vote system, with direct election for three-quarters of the seats and "topping-up" with additional members chosen from the unsuccessful candidates according to their party and their percentage of the constituency vote, thus eliminating party lists altogether and also retaining single-member constituencies of reasonable size (about 85,000 on average as against 64,000).[23] The directly elected members would be elected as at present, though it seems to me that they ought to be elected by the alternative vote so as to give candidates of minority parties a better chance of improving their poll and so becoming additional members. A threshold of five per cent. of the overall vote would be set, below which no party could obtain additional members. Nearly all variants have some initial hurdle of this kind to prevent fragmentation of parties.

A strong rival to all these devices is the single transferable vote,[24] which is preferred by many expert psepholo-

---

[22] See the Blake Commission, paras. 111–121; R. Holme, *A Democracy Which Works* (Parliamentary Democracy Trust, undated), an account of the West German system.
[23] para. 120.
[24] See the Blake Commission, paras. 98–110. For the Royal Commission's scheme for 100 House of Commons seats, see Cd. 9044 (1918). For the scheme used in the university constituencies, see S.R. & O. 1918, No. 1348, made under Representation of the People Act 1918, s.36.

gists. This is the system used in the university constituencies between 1918 and 1948, in Northern Ireland from 1973 for elections to the Assembly, the Constitutional Convention, the European Assembly, and district councils, and in the Irish Republic since its foundation. It is a complex scheme which has the merits of avoiding party lists and making it possible for voters to discriminate between different candidates of the same party. It does however require very large multi-member constituencies, and in many people's eyes this is a serious disadvantage—though it should not be forgotten that two- or three-member constituencies were in use in Britain before 1885. It is thought that an average constituency would have about five members, so that its average size would be in excess of 300,000 and there might be say 15 candidates on the ballot paper. The voter can list his preferences freely. A quota is fixed for each constituency by a simple formula related to the number of votes cast and the number of seats. If the votes cast are 300,000 and there are five seats, the quota is 300,000 divided by six plus one equals 50,001. Any candidate who attains this quota of first preferences is automatically elected. Any surplus votes in excess of the quota are transferred to other candidates in proportions according to the second preferences on the winning candidate's ballot papers, taken as a whole. The process is repeated if necessary, and if on any count no candidate attains the quota the bottom candidate is eliminated and his second preferences are allotted to the others. Thus wasted votes are minimised and the voter can pick and choose between candidates offering a wide choice of policies. The system is designed for a sophisticated electorate, but in a large country the size of the constituencies means weakening the personal tie between constituent and member. That objection may not be decisive since in reality voters mostly for parties rather than for the individual candidates. And this is the one and only proportional system which has actually been used in the United Kingdom to a small extent. My own belief is that the single transferable vote is an unduly complex mechanism for the British electorate as a whole, and that the majority of the Blake Commission were right in preferring the additional member system, under which elections would be conducted almost exactly as they are now and constituencies would not be much larger.

SELECTION OF CANDIDATES

Since voting is mostly, as Professor de Smith put it, "a ritualistic affirmation of support for (or hostility to) one of the two main parties," it is important that the official party candidates should fairly represent general opinion in the party, and that the procedure for selecting them should be fair and democratic. Here once again our constitutional law leaves much to be desired—or rather it leaves everything to be desired, since it makes no provision whatever. Consequently there is much complaint that supporters of the parties are given very little voice in the selection of candidates, who may be chosen by party caucuses dominated by small and unrepresentative groups, who will often be the most active party members. So this is yet another factor aggravating the polarisation and extremism which tend to flourish in a legal vacuum. The principal parties have their selection procedures and in some cases there is a poll of party members, but none of this is regulated by law. In the United States, on the other hand, the law provides elaborately for primary elections so that voters can exercise a choice, and this is rightly regarded as an essential part of democracy. The British system (or non-system) fails utterly to recognise that in a great many cases the selection of the candidate is in substance the election itself, since there are so many safe seats in which a party's official candidate can be sure of winning. These are the rotten boroughs of our own time, almost as undemocratic in some cases as those which were swept away in 1832 and there are a great many of them. The Blake Commission looked at this problem too and recommended a system of direct choice of candidates by party members in a secret ballot financed by public funds and required by law as a condition of nomination in a party's name. Surely we must recognise that selection of party candidates is a vital part of our electoral system, that it is open to abuse and that its regulation by law is indispensable.

THE SECOND CHAMBER

When there are such serious undemocratic elements in the composition of the House of Commons it is all the more important to maintain the check, such as it is, provided by the House of Lords. One would certainly like to see the fulfilment of the intention declared in the preamble of the Parliament Act 1911, that the House of Lords should be reorganised on a popular instead of a hereditary basis. Other democratic countries have created successful second chambers and it cannot be beyond the ability of this country to do the same. Here again, unfortunately, is a matter on which there seems to be little hope of reform from within Parliament itself. If the House of Commons were itself more truly representative, perhaps the prospects would improve. Meanwhile some constitutional counterpoise to the House of Commons seems highly desirable, and the one that exists is better than none at all. The top priority, if my diagnosis is correct, should be to reform the electoral system for the House of Commons. That is where the power resides and that is where true popular representation is most urgently needed. Until this is done the pot should cease calling the kettle black.

*   *   *

The epilogue to this lecture can be short and sharp. If

we really believe that our democracy should be representative and responsive, we must admit that our constitutional law is gravely inadequate. It fails to provide for the fair distribution of seats, for fair results in elections and for fair selection of candidates. Too few lawyers, as I venture to think, have raised their voices for the necessary reforms, which ought especially to concern those whose profession is justice. When Lord Byers opened a debate in the House of Lords on the political and electoral system in 1976 he said that there was a direct causal relationship between our social and economic crises and the system of electing members of the House of Commons.[25] I am sure that I am not the only person who believes that he was right.

[25] 368 H.L. Deb. 87 (February 11, 1976).

Chapter 3

LEGISLATION

A Defective System

Among the numerous and deep-seated defects of our method of legislation two which stand out, to my mind, are at opposite extremes of the constitutional spectrum. At the lower end is the mere mechanism, which I think most lawyers would say is in a state of acute malfunction, producing laws which are excessive in quantity and deficient in quality. At the higher, or at any rate the more theoretical, end of the spectrum is the inability of the legislature, as is generally supposed, to enact any system of entrenched fundamental rights, such as other countries enjoy. Both these failings can be blamed on the dogma of Parliamentary sovereignty, but in opposite ways. The first arises from legislative omnipotence and the ease with which governments can manipulate it. The second arises from legislative impotence and the doctrine that no Parliament can bind its successors. Most of this lecture will be devoted to the second problem, but I will begin with a few words about the first.

The technique of legislation is, I suppose, the subject of more objurgation and malediction by lawyers than any other aspect of their profession. In 1975 it was studied by a strong committee appointed by the government and presided over by Sir David (now Lord) Renton.[1] They made 121 recommendations. In the aggregate these are of great importance and potential benefit, but none of them can be described as radical. Among the more

[1] *The Preparation of Legislation*, Cmnd. 6053 (1975).

notable were the recommendations that advice on draft
Bills should be sought from specialists in the relevant
branches of law; that statements of principle should be
encouraged; that earlier Acts should be amended by the
textual rather than the referential method where convenience permits; and that the structure and language of
statutes should be kept under continuous review by the
Statute Law Committee, a Lord Chancellor's committee
of eminent lawyers and experts which was first constituted over 100 years ago. There were many other
minor recommendations, for example that there should
be no ban on the use of a full stop in the middle of a
section or subsection. While on that level I would like to
add a 122nd recommendation, which is that Acts should
not be given misleading short titles. The Ministry of
Social Security Act 1966 was so unsuitably entitled that
seven years later it was rechristened the Supplementary
Benefit Act 1966; this was done by subsection 18 of
the section 99 of the Social Security Act 1973, and great
must have been the confusion caused in legal minds
before this obscure provision was tracked down. Another
case is the Unfair Contract Terms Act 1977, which
contains provisions about notices disclaiming liability in
situations where there is no contract of any kind.
Another is the Welsh Language Act 1967, which provides that in Acts of Parliament "England" no longer
includes Wales, though this important change has
nothing to do with the Welsh language. Titles like these
are traps not only for the unwary but for the wary also.
All lawyers should support the efforts of the Statute Law
Society, an independent body which is helping to mobi-
lise legal opinion and to give this subject the attention it
deserves.

Perhaps the most shocking feature of our legislative
process is the way in which Parliamentary scrutiny is
eliminated on the pretext of shortage of time. When the

Scotland Bill was before Parliament in 1978, 58 of its 87 clauses and 14 of its 17 schedules were passed over without discussion in the House of Commons, including all the financial clauses which of course the House of Lords could not discuss either.[2] Yet this was revolutionary constitutional legislation—abortive though it proved in the end. It cannot be an adequate excuse to say that there is no time for proper consideration of important Bills. Admittedly the party system has distorted the constitution to such an extent that most legislation could more accurately be said to be enacted by the government than by Parliament. There is truth, unfortunately, in Lord Hailsham's charge that we have allowed the constitution to become an elective dictatorship.[3] If Parliament is no longer willing or able to give proper attention to legislation, we should perhaps consider whether some new body ought to be invented for this purpose. In France the vetting of draft legislation is an important function of the Conseil d'Etat, to which the government is required by the constitution to submit its Bills before introducing them in the legislature.[4] The Conseil d'Etat will criticise provisions which are objectionable in principle, and also bad drafting. Government Bills are thus vetted by an independent and highly professional body, and not merely by those who are in a hurry to push them through Parliament. The same applies to government decrees and regulations, so that the whole technique of legislation is under the Conseil's superintendence. I am not myself one of those who advocate an administrative

[2] For a strong protest by Lord Wilberforce on another occasion, see 358 H.L. Deb. 433 (March 13, 1975).
[3] *Elective Dictatorship* (1976); *The Dilemma of Democracy* (1978), Chap. xx. R. H. S. Crossman in his introduction to Bagehot, *The English Constitution*, (1963) draws similar conclusions.
[4] See Brown and Garner, *French Administrative Law* (2nd ed.), p. 32 (now 3rd ed., p. 42); Rendel, *The Administrative Functions of the French Conseil d'Etat*; and note in [1970] Pub. L. 217.

court like the judicial side of the Conseil. But an
institution modelled on its administrative side, which
could superintend the technique of legislation without
itself being under the thumb of the government, is to my
mind something which we need much more.

THE PROBLEM OF ENTRENCHMENT

Now I want to turn to quite a different legislative
problem: how to achieve the entrenchment of fundamental rights. May I first make it clear that I intend to resist
the temptation to launch into all the pros and cons of a
Bill of Rights, now such a popular subject of speculation.
Several of my Hamlyn predecessors have favoured one,
notably Lord Scarman and Sir Norman Anderson. For
my own part I will say merely that I am firmly on their
side, and on the side of the majority of the House of
Lords who have four times called for the incorporation
into our law of the European Convention on Human
Rights.[5] What I will attempt is to supply the missing legal
link between the wish and the fulfilment. For none of the
distinguished lawyers who have advocated entrenched
Bills of Rights—and they include Lord Hailsham, Lord
Salmon and Lord Scarman—have explained how
entrenchment could be made to work consistently with
the dogma of parliamentary sovereignty. I approach this
now as a purely technical problem of legislation: how can
our legislative machinery be made to deliver these particular goods? In any normal situation there is no need
for any such question, since Parliament is omnipotent.
But the one inherent limit on its omnipotence, which is
the consequence of that omnipotence itself, is that the
Parliament of today cannot fetter the Parliament of

---

[5] See 403 H.L. Deb. 915 (December 6, 1979): Bill of Rights Bill passed.
A private member's Bill in the House of Commons failed to obtain a
second reading on February 6, 1987.

tomorrow with any sort of permanent restraint, so that entrenched provisions are impossible.

That, at any rate, appears to be the view of the legal establishment. It was accepted by the Select Committee of the House of Lords which in 1978 reported on the possibility of enacting a Bill of Rights incorporating the European Convention. The Committee employed a specialist adviser to guide them on this question, and he advised them, in a very lucid paper, that the judicial authorities led to the clear conclusion that there was no way in which a Bill of Rights could be made immune from amendment or repeal by a subsequent Act.[6] Entrenched provisions, such as clauses alterable only by two-thirds majorities, or after approval in a referendum could not therefore be legally effective in the United Kingdom.[7] A footnote informs us that Lord Diplock, Lord Scarman and Lord Wilberforce were in general agreement with this conclusion. This weighty consensus was qualified only by a reservation on the part of Lord Hailsham, but the Committee observe that that reservation was based more on hope that the specialist adviser's view might prove wrong than on any confident expectation that it would.

Lord Hailsham had himself categorically adopted the establishment view in the debates of 1972 on the European Communities Act. That Act, as we all know, has attempted to entrench the law of the European Communities in the most absolute way possible, providing that the European law is to prevail over "any enactment passed or to be passed, other than one contained in this part of this Act."[8] So Parliament has ordained that every future Act of Parliament as well as every past Act, is to

[6] Evidence to Select Committee on a Bill of Rights, H.L. 276 of May 17, 1977. p. 1 (D. Rippengal).
[7] Report of the Select Committee, H.L. 176 of May 24, 1978, p. 22.
[8] European Communities Act 1972, s.2(4).

give way in case of conflict. There is nothing here about two-thirds majorities or approval by referendum. Parliament has attempted to bind its successors unconditionally. Yet the same ministers who were piloting the Bill through Parliament maintained that Parliament's ultimate sovereignty remained intact for the simple reason that it was indestructible by legislation. They used this proposition to resist an opposition amendment to the effect that the supremacy of Parliament should remain unaffected. This was unnecessary, they argued, because Parliament is bound to remain supreme anyway and no restriction on its powers, or on the manner of their exercise, is constitutionally possible. Sir Geoffrey Howe in the House of Commons[9] and Lord Hailsham in the House of Lords[10] quoted from an article of mine, my solitary contribution to the arguments over sovereignty, published many years ago. The clue which led to it was perhaps its mention by Lord Denning M.R. in the case in which Mr. Raymond Blackburn unsuccessfully contested the constitutionality of this country's joining the European Communities.[11] I had said[12]:

> "If no statute can establish the rule that the courts obey Acts of Parliament, similarly no statute can alter or abolish that rule. The rule is above and beyond the reach of statute . . . because it is itself the source of the authority of statute. This puts it into a class by itself as a rule of common law, and the apparent paradox that it is unalterable by Parliament turns out to be a truism. . . . Legislation owes its authority to the rule: the rule does not owe its authority to legislation."

[9] 840 H.C. Deb. 628 (July 5, 1972).
[10] 334 H.L. Deb. 912 (August 7, 1972).
[11] *Blackburn* v. *Att.-Gen.* [1971] 1 W.L.R. 1037.
[12] [1955] C.L.J. 187.

This was merely one way of expressing two obvious facts. The first is that in every legal system there must be a basic rule or rules for identifying a valid piece of legislation, whether we call it the grundnorm, like Kelsen, or the ultimate legal principle, like Salmond, or the rule of recognition, like Professor Hart. The second obvious fact is that this grundnorm, or whatever we call it, lies in the keeping of the judges and it is for them to say what they will recognise as effective legislation. For this one purpose Parliament's powers of giving orders to the judges are ineffective. It is futile for Parliament to command the judges not to recognise the validity of future Acts of Parliament which conflict with a Bill of Rights, or with European Community law, if the judges habitually accept that later Acts prevail over earlier Acts and are determined to go on doing so. In this one fundamental matter it is the judges who are sovereign.

That, in very condensed form, is the theory which underlies the view of the legal establishment. In my humble opinion that view is unquestionably sound. There is an abundance of judicial authority for it and a total dearth of authority against it.[13] But nevertheless I hope to persuade you that it need not prevent the effective entrenchment of a Bill of Rights or of anything else that we may wish to establish as fundamental law.

RIVAL THEORIES

Before coming to the point, if I may keep you in suspense, I must face up to various rival theories. It will be convenient, first of all, to deal with those based upon the Parliament Acts of 1911 and 1949. Professor de Smith maintained that by these Acts Parliament had redefined itself for particular purposes: the sovereign legislature of Queen, Lords and Commons had provided

[13] See the articles referred to in nn. 6 and 12, above.

an optional alternative consisting of Queen and Commons only; and this new body could legislate in accordance with the Acts for all purposes other than prolongation of the life of Parliament. Such legislation, he said, was primary and not delegated; yet he accepted that if it purported to prolong the life of Parliament it would be a nullity.[14] With this last point I fully agree, but I cannot square it with the notion that legislation enacted under the Parliament Acts is primary. The acid test of primary legislation, surely, is that it is accepted by the courts at its own face value, without needing support from any superior authority. But an Act passed by Queen and Commons only has no face value of its own. As Coke put it in *The Prince's Case*, "If an Act be penned, that the King with the assent of the Lords, or with the assent of the Commons, it is no Act of Parliament for three ought to assent to it *scil* the King, the Lords and the Commons."[15] An Act of Queen and Commons alone is accepted by the courts only because it is authorised by the Parliament Acts—and indeed it is required to recite that it is passed "in accordance with the Parliament Acts 1911 and 1949 and by authority of the same."[16] This is the hall-mark of subordinate legislation, and I do not understand how it is possible to disagree with Professor Hood Phillips when he says that this is the correct classification.[17] The importance of this academic controversy is that if the redefinition theory were sound it would provide an easy mechanism for entrenchment. Parliament could, by an ordinary Act, redefine itself for the purpose of amending (say) a Bill of Rights so that the competent legislature for this purpose

[14] *Constitutional and Administrative Law* (3rd ed.), pp. 86–90, replaced by 5th ed., pp. 100–104.

[15] (1606) 8 Co. Rep. 1, 20(*b*).

[16] Parliament Acts 1911, s.4(1); 1949, s.2(2).

[17] *Constitutional and Administrative Law* (6th ed.) pp. 89–90, (now 7th ed., p. 90).

was one which could only act by (say) two-thirds majorities. Parliament could of course pass such a statute, but how could it prevent itself, in its ordinary bicameral form, from repealing it? The redefinition theory seems to lead nowhere for the present purpose, and I feel bound to agree with the commentator who criticised it as unacceptable.[18]

Another school of thought maintains that the judges will accept entrenchment without further ado and will spontaneously uphold any restrictions laid down by an earlier Parliament as to how later Parliaments shall enact statutes. This bold assertion has been made only by academics and they might be described as the "manner and form" school—for they maintain that there is a distinction between the substance of legislation and the manner and form in which it has to be passed. As to the substance, they admit, every future Parliament remains sovereign. But as to the manner and form, they say, future Parliaments must legislate in accordance with the existing law, and if that law requires two-thirds majorities in Parliament or perhaps a referendum, an Act which does not obey these requirements will not be recognised by the courts as a valid Act of Parliament. Their watchwords "manner and form" are the words of the Colonial Laws Validity Act 1865 which were crucial in the well known Privy Council case of *Att.-Gen. for New South Wales* v. *Trethowan*.[19] In that case it was held that an Act of the New South Wales Parliament abolishing the Legislative Council was invalid since it had not been approved by a referendum as an earlier Act of the same Parliament had stipulated. New South Wales in those days was in a state of legal subordination to Britain, and since the Colonial Laws Validity Act laid down that colonial laws of the kind in question must be

[18] P. N. Mirfield in (1979) 95 L.Q.R. 36, 47.
[19] [1932] A.C. 526.

passed in the manner and form required by the law for the time being in force, the result was inevitable. Ignoring this decisive fact, the "manner and form" enthusiasts seize upon the *Trethowan* case as showing that a Parliament can bind its successors as to the manner and form of future legislation, and they contend that the result would be just the same in Britain if Parliament were, say, to enact that the House of Lords should not be abolished without a referendum and then a later Act, without a referendum, attempted to abolish it: this second Act, they say, would be held void. I have drawn a good deal of powder and shot upon myself for pointing out the simple fallacies upon which the "manner and form" position rests—a whole appendix from Sir Ivor Jennings[20] and an accusation from Professor Heuston that my reaction to it was that of a mindless automaton.[21] But, in the end, what is the substance of their argument? It is simply their prediction, made with varying degrees of dogmatism, that the judges will, or should, enforce restrictions about manner and form and abandon their clear and settled rule that the traditional manner and form is what counts.[21a] But if it is vain for Parliament to command the judges to transfer their allegiance to some new system of legislation if the judges are resolved to remain loyal to the old one, it is still more vain for professors to assert that they should. The judicial loyalty is the foundation of the legal system and, at the same time, a political fact.

[20] *The Law and the Constitution* (5th ed.), p. 318.
[21] *Essays in Constitutional Law* (2nd ed.). p. 24. The "manner and form" theory is decisively rejected in Mr. Rippengal's memorandum (n. 6, above). Professor de Smith (as n. 14, above) seems to accept it at p. 88, n. 107 (3rd ed.), and p. 101, n. 107 (5th ed.).
[21a] They may now claim the support of three of the seven judges of the Supreme Court of Canada in *Re Singh and Minister of Employment and Immigration* (1985) 17 D.L.R. (4th) 422. But the passage (at 441) is of three lines only and devoid of reasons. The three judges held that the rights conferred by the Canadian Bill of Rights 1960 prevailed over later inconsistent provisions of the Immigration Act 1976.

This is the reality which the "manner and form" school fail to appreciate.

JUDICIAL ADJUSTMENTS

I have never suggested that no shift in judicial loyalty is possible. One has only to look at the shifts which took place in seventeenth-century England, in eighteenth-century America and in the twentieth-century dissolution of the British Empire, latterly in particular in Zimbabwe. These shifts are revolutions, breaks in continuity and in the legal pedigree of legislative power. Even without such discontinuity there might be a shift of judicial loyalty if we take into account the dimension of time. Suppose that Parliament were to enact a Bill of Rights entrenched by a clause saying that it was to be amended or repealed only by Acts certified to be passed by two-thirds majorities in both Houses. Suppose also that Parliament scrupulously observed this rule for 50 or 100 years, so that no conflicting legislation came before the courts. Meanwhile new generations of judges might come to accept that there had been a new constitutional settlement based on common consent and long usage, and that the old doctrine of sovereignty was ancient history, to be classed with the story of the Witenagemot, Bonham's case, the Rump, Barebones' Parliament and the Jacobite pretenders. The judges would then be adjusting their doctrine to the facts of constitutional life, as they have done throughout history.

Something like this may indeed be happening in New Zealand. There it was provided in the Electoral Act 1956 that certain "reserved provisions" were to be repealed or amended only by a vote of 75 per cent. of the House of Representatives or after approval in a referendum. At the time it was accepted that this provision could itself be repealed by an ordinary Act. Now that it has been respected for many years it seems possible that a kind of moral entrenchment may have been achieved, and it has been seriously suggested that legislation infringing it might be put in question by the Governor-General refusing assent to it.[22] But one can imagine the crisis which this might precipitate.

JUDICIAL ACCEPTANCE?

There is another school of thought which, without following the "manner and form" school, postulates, or at any rate hopes, that the judges might accept and enforce entrenched clauses without needing a century or so to get used to the idea. Lord Scarman, in his Hamlyn Lectures of 1974,[23] made a strong case for entrenchment as a necessary feature of a Bill of Rights and a new constitutional settlement. He acknowledged "the helplessness of the law in face of the legislative sovereignty of Parliament," but he did not see why this should be so basic as to be unalterable; and he observed that both British history and American experience showed that the necessary adjustment could be made. He pointed to the limitations on sovereignty asserted by Coke and Holt, who both held that Acts of Parliament might be void if contrary to common right and reason or the principles of natural justice. He also made an interesting reference to Coke's dictum that Acts of Parliament were not binding on the Court of King's Bench because it represented the King himself, *coram ipso Rege*,[24] difficult though it is to imagine counsel having much success with such a submission today. In the nineteenth century rigid-minded lawyers, such as Lord Campbell, scoffed at the idea that

---

[22] K. J. Keith in *Thirteen Facets: Essays to Celebrate the Silver Jubilee of Queen Elizabeth II* (Wellington, 1978), pp. 11–12.
[23] *English Law—The New Dimension*, pp. 15–21.
[24] *Foster's Case* (1615) 11 Co. Rep. 56b. 65a.

there could be limited sovereignty.[25] Lord Scarman's point, however, is simply that if great lawyers have supported it in the past, they might equally well do so again in the future. Yet the problem still remains, how to bring that about by legislation?

The European Communities Act 1972, by providing that European law should prevail over future Acts of Parliament, has attempted to entrench the whole of European law in the most absolute fashion—although, as I have mentioned, its sponsors made it clear that they did not really believe that it could. In a published lecture Mr. J.-P. Warner Q.C., Advocate-General at the European Court in Luxembourg, said that he believed that there were sound arguments for holding that the entrenchment was effective.[26] He did not say what they were, or join issue with the ministerial spokesmen who maintained the contrary. But he very fairly observed that it really would be lamentable if British constitutional law were held to be so rigid, and so divorced from reality, as to make it impossible for the United Kingdom to honour its obligations under the Community Treaties. A contradictory opinion had fallen not long before from Lord Denning M.R. in the *Felixstowe Docks* case, where he had said that if the private Bill about the docks was enacted by Parliament, that would dispose of all argument about the "abuse of a dominant position" under the Treaty of Rome: for the courts would then have to "abide by the statute without regard to the Treaty at all."[27]

[25] See *Lives of the Chief Justices* (Vol. 1), p. 341 on the "foolish doctrine" of *Dr. Bonham's Case* (1610) 8 Co. Rep. 113b, 118a which "ought to have been laughed at."

[26] (1977) 93 L.Q.R. 349, 365. The author is now the Hon. Mr. Justice Warner.

[27] *Felixstowe Docks & Ry. Co.* v. *British Transport Docks Board* [1976] 2 C.M.L.R. 655. In *Macarthys Ltd.* v. *Smith* [1979] I.C.R. 174 Lord Denning adds that the intention to override the Treaty must be clear.

There is one thing on which all the contenders engaged on this juristic battleground would agree. This is that it is absurd that important public discussions, such as the House of Lords' debate on the proposal for enacting a Bill of Rights, should have to be held on the assumption that entrenchment is impossible. Yet the Select Committee, whose Report was the subject of the debate, treated it as clear that no provision for special majorities or for referendums or for placing any restriction upon amendment or repeal by the traditional procedure could be made legally effective. With the greatest respect to the Committee, I would agree that no such restriction would be effective if merely enacted in the normal manner, except possibly after a transitional interval too long and uncertain to be of practical interest. But it does not follow that there is no constitutional means for producing the desired result. It may seem paradoxical that there is any legal mechanism more effective than an ordinary Act of Parliament. But when we are dealing with the fundamental doctrine under which the judges declare what statutory directions they will accept, we are dealing with a unique principle which is more than just an ordinary rule of law. Not only is it part of the network of legal rules: it is also the peg from which the network hangs.

ATTEMPTS AT ENTRENCHMENT

Theoretical difficulties have not prevented Parliament from attempting to fetter its successors from time to time. The earliest example that I know is the Act entitled Confirmation of the Charters of 1369,[28] which provided:

> ". . . it is assented and accorded that the Great Charter and the Charter of the Forest be holden and kept in all points; and if there be any statute made to the contrary, it shall be holden for none."

[28] 43 Ed. 3, c. 1.

Another instance is the Act of 1495[29] designed to prevent
the attainder of those who gave allegiance to the King
reigning *de facto* for the time being, in case he should
later be held a usurper:

> "if any act or acts or other process of the law
> hereafter happen to be made contrary to this ordi-
> nance, then that act or acts or other process of the
> law . . . should be void."

The vicissitudes of fifteenth-century politics not
unnaturally prompted legislators to strive for some element of stability by enacting permanent safeguards.
Unfortunately we have no case in which a court was
called upon to apply this unsophisticated effort at
entrenchment. But Coke and Blackstone were both quite
certain that all such attempts were ineffective. Blackstone elegantly cites a passage from Cicero's letters
which indicates that in the Roman republic lawyers were
familiar with the same doctrine.[30] The translation reads:

> "Clodius, as you know, attached sanctions to his Bill
> to make it almost or quite impossible for it to be
> invalidated either by the Senate or by the Assembly.
> But precedent shows you that such sanctions have
> never been observed in the case of laws to be
> repealed. Otherwise it would be virtually impossible
> to repeal any law, for there is none but protects
> itself by putting difficulties in the way of repeal. But
> when a law is repealed, the provision against repeal
> is repealed at the same time."

I need not linger over the Acts for securing the church
establishments in Scotland and Ireland, which, according
to the Acts of Union, were to be for ever observed as

[29] 11. Hen. 7, c. 1.
[30] Comm. i, 90, citing Letters to Atticus, bk. iii, no. 23.

fundamental and essential conditions. Those solemn
enactments did not prevent later statutory amendments.[31]
Though there is a clear case for regarding the Treaty of
Union as a constitutional convention, intended to establish fundamental law, the truth is that the Treaty was
made too early, and the argument has been raised too
late, for this reasoning to be acceptable to the courts.
But Parliament undoubtedly purported to fetter its successors in the Statute of Westminster 1931, by providing
that no Act of Parliament was in future to extend to a
Dominion unless it declared in the Act itself that the
Dominion had requested and consented thereto. And we
all know Lord Sankey's trenchant comment, that Parliament could, as a matter of abstract law, repeal or
disregard the requirement of request and consent; "But
that is theory and has no relation to realities."[32] To the
realm of unreality also belong the proposals made to the
Royal Commission on the Constitution by Jersey and the
Isle of Man, that their relationship with the United
Kingdom should be embodied in statutes which would
provide that they should not be amended or repealed
without their consent.[33]

But there is a very direct relation to realities in the
European Communities Act 1972, which provides that
European Community law shall prevail over all enactments "passed or to be passed." The reality here is that
it is virtually certain that sooner or later some Act passed
after 1972 will be found to be in conflict with community
law, as has now happened in several of the other member
countries. Lord Denning has already gone on record, as I
have mentioned, with the dictum that the courts of this
country would then have to obey the later Act without

[31] By the Universities (Scotland) Act 1853 and the Irish Church Act
1869.
[32] *British Coal Corp.* v. *The King* [1935] A.C. 500, 520.
[33] Report of the Royal Commission on the Constitution, Cmnd. 5460
(1973), para. 1417.

regard to the Treaty of Rome. When the Bill was before Parliament in 1972 I ventured to point out how this potential conflict might be avoided by subordinating all future legislation to Community law by some short and suitable addition to the conventional words of enactment.[34] Nothing of that kind having been done, a profound puzzle has simply been bequeathed to the judges.

THE NEED FOR A SOLUTION

With these problems impending, surely it is time this country grew up constitutionally and stopped mumbling feebly that nothing can be done. I think that this is part of what Lord Wilberforce had in mind when he said, during the debates on the Scotland Bill, that it was time to put an end to "constitutional anarchy," or alternatively "non-constitutional despotism," and to start taking the constitution seriously.[35] In the present context, it is time that we took the trouble to discover how to provide ourselves with the legal mechanisms which virtually all other comparable countries have. Whether we want entrenched provisions or whether we do not, we ought at least to be able to make a choice on the merits, instead of being told by constitutional pundits that no choice is open to us. Whether the argument is about a Bill of Rights, the European Convention on Human Rights, or the law of the European Communities, the whole debate is distorted unless we have the full range of options which is open to any country which wants to establish, for the first time, new fundamental laws. The absurdity of saying that we have not the option of entrenchment becomes all the greater if we remember to how many other countries we have ourselves given it. In the new countries of the British Commonwealth it has

---

[34] *The Times*, April 18, 1972, p. 14.
[35] 390 H.L. Deb. 1094 (April 18, 1978).

been standard practice to include in their constitutions the familiar kind of restrictions on constitutional amendment which require special majorities such as two-thirds; and part and parcel of the constitution is commonly a catalogue of fundamental rights. If they wish to entrench anything further, all they have to do is to obtain a constitutional amendment. And they may have power, as for example India has (subject to ratification by not less than half the States), to amend the amendment provision itself, so that they can alter the degree of entrenchment and make it as rigid or as pliable as they wish.[36] So they enjoy all possible options.

MUST THERE BE A REVOLUTION?

A primary question to explore, in approaching our own problem, is whether it is indispensable to have a revolution, or its equivalent, before the traditional doctrine of sovereignty can be changed. Constitutional restraints are the natural product of revolutions, since there is then a clean break with the past and any rules of any kind can be adopted for the future. A constituent assembly may be convened without any legal antecedents and the very fact of its irregularity gives authority to the constitution that it adopts. Part of our difficulty in Britain is that we have not had a fresh start of this kind since 1688, and that was a century before the era of written constitutions. The interesting question is, must there necessarily be a legal break with the past in order that a different principle of sovereignty may be established? Certainly that has been so in most of the cases which come to mind, and I include among them all the transfers of sovereignty to the newly independent countries of the British Commonwealth. For one must not be deceived by legal camouflage. When the Ghana Independence Act

[36] Constitution of India, art. 368.

(for example) was passed in 1957, the Constitution of Ghana having been duly created by Order in Council beforehand, there was in fact just as clean a break with the British legal connection as there was when the Constitution of the United States of America was adopted in 1787 after the successful rebellion.[37] On paper the Constitution of Ghana had a legal pedigree deriving from Britain. But in reality Ghana was launched into independence and her judges would in future have to solve her constitutional problems on their own.

Over twenty years beforehand South Africa had made the same discovery when she severed her connection in 1934, proclaiming by statute that she was an independent sovereign state—a step which she was fully entitled to take, so far as British law was concerned, under the Statute of Westminster 1931. Then the question arose, what about the entrenched clauses? South Africa had not adopted any new constitution in 1934, so continued to live under the constitution of 1909, imposed from Westminster, which provided that certain matters, including the electoral rights of the Cape coloured voters, should be changed only by a two-thirds majority of both Houses of Parliament sitting together. But the government claimed that after 1934 they could be changed by an Act passed by simple majorities in the two Houses separately, since the South African Parliament was now sovereign, and, it was asserted, could no more be bound by any earlier enactment than could the sovereign Parliament of the United Kingdom. Constitutional lawyers then disputed this question as if there was a legal path leading to the correct solution. But in fact there was no such path: there was a new situation, in which only the judges could say what they would now recognise as a valid Act of the new sovereign legislature. In fact they

---

[37] The right of appeal to the Judicial Committee of the Privy Council, retained until 1960, made no difference.

elected to retain the entrenched clauses.[38] But had they decided the contrary, as indeed they had done in one earlier case, this would have been no less justifiable in terms of constitutionality. Notwithstanding the statutory camouflage provided both in London and Pretoria, there had been a revolution, legally speaking, and the judges were called upon to lay down the fundamental law of the new legal system, as it were in a vacuum.

Despite all the legal accoutrements, a revolution of some kind, in the sense of a break in legal continuity, seems to be lurking in any situation where there is a shift of the seat or the forms of sovereign legislative power. Lord Hailsham has written that to produce it in this country would require "a political crisis far more serious than anything which has faced us hitherto."[39] And even after such a cataclysm doubts might remain until the courts had decided cases, since only they can say whom in the last resort they will obey. To meet these difficulties Messrs. Wallington and McBride suggest, in their book *Civil Liberties and a Bill of Rights*,[40] that the Lord Chancellor could persuade the judges of the House of Lords to issue a practice statement, like their pronouncement of 1966 about precedent, to the effect that they would disallow future legislation conflicting with a new Bill of Rights. I feel bound to agree with the advice given to Lord Wade's Committee, that the notion that the House of Lords would seek to make a fundamental constitutional change in such a way is hardly sustainable.[41] And I would say the same about the role assigned to the Lord Chancellor. But at least the suggestion is aimed at the right point. It is the minds of the judges

---

[38] *Harris* v. *Minister of the Interior* 1952 (2) S.A. 428; [1952] 12 T.L.R. 1245.
[39] *The Times*, May 20, 1975, p. 14.
[40] p. 86.
[41] As n. 6, above para. 12.

which require to be adjusted, and to pass statutes merely telling them to adjust themselves is futile.

THE EASY WAY OUT

After all this build-up my own suggestion will seem, I fear, very simple and obvious. But I believe it to be the one to which logic inexorably leads. All that need be done in order to entrench any sort of fundamental law is to secure its recognition in the judicial oath of office. The only trouble at present is that the existing form of oath gives no assurance of obedience to statutes binding later Parliaments. But there is every assurance that if the judges undertake upon their oath to act in some particular way they will do so. If we should wish to adopt a new form of constitution, therefore, all that need be done is to put the judges under oath to enforce it. An Act of Parliament could be passed to discharge them from their former oaths, if that were thought necessary, and to require them to be resworn in the new terms. All the familiar problems of sovereignty then disappear: a fresh start has been made; the doctrine that no Parliament can bind its successors becomes ancient history; and the new fundamental law is secured by a judiciary sworn to uphold it.

If critics should object that this would be a mere piece of manipulation and a subversive tampering with the status of the judges, I would meet them head on by denying the validity of the objection. It is only because we are so habituated to having no constitution at all that our minds can move in such grooves. There is no need to assume that there is only one kind of judge and only one form of oath. In fact, it is the most natural and normal procedure to relate the judicial oath specifically to any new fundamental law that is to be established. Article VI of the Constitution of the United States provides that judicial as well as executive officers both of the United

States and of the States shall be bound by oath or affirmation to support the Constitution. In the Constitution of India a variety of oaths for judges, ministers, and members of Parliament are set out in the Third Schedule, and all are required to swear fidelity to the Constitution and the judges must swear to uphold it. There are similar requirements in the Constitution of Malaysia. But throughout history oaths have been used to secure revolutionary changes, such as the Reformation in the time of Henry VIII and the Revolution in the time of William III. William III, when he accepted the crown at the Revolution, took security for his legal position as sovereign by appointing new judges who swore allegiance to him personally,[42] just as today the judges of the Supreme Court of Judicature take the oath of allegiance and the judicial oath in the forms prescribed by the Promissory Oaths Act 1868, which name the reigning sovereign. The one thing that our rudimentary constitution guarantees in this way is the personality of the sovereign. If we want to guarantee something else, such as a Bill of Rights or some particular entrenched clauses, all we have to do is extend the same security to them.

This is, as it appears to me, the one and only way in which we can take command of our constitution without having to wait for some sort of political revolution, which is most unlikely to arrive just when we want it, and without having to contrive some artificial legal discontinuity. Professor Hood Phillips, in his book on the Reform of the Constitution, suggests that Parliament would have to abdicate or transfer its powers, with or without the intervention of a constituent assembly.[43] But merely by a change in the judicial oath a new judicial attitude can be created, and that is all that is needed.

---

[42] Except for Atkyns and Powell JJ. who were reappointed: Campbell, *Lives of the Chief Justices* (3rd ed.), Vol. 2, p. 381.

[43] p. 157, adding that new judicial oaths would be necessary.

Fundamentally the question simply is, what will the judges recognise as a valid Act of Parliament? If they solemnly undertake to recognise a new grundnorm and to refuse validity to Acts of Parliament which conflict with a Bill of Rights or other entrenched clauses, that is the best possible assurance that the entrenchment will work. Always in the end we come back to the ultimate legal reality: an Act of Parliament is valid only if the judges say it is, and only they can say what the rules for its validity are.

The logic could be pressed further by including in the judicial oath an undertaking to pay no attention to future legislation affecting the oath unless passed by (say) two-thirds majorities in Parliament. It could be pressed further still if the undertaking were to pay no attention to any such legislation of any kind. All that that would mean, however, would be that whole benches of new judges would have to be found to replace the old ones, just as at William III's accession, if and when the time for the second revolution arrived. Cheering as this prospect might be to the Bar, it is not a situation which one would wish to provoke. I mention it only because, theoretically at least, it seems to represent the ultimate in possible entrenchment. There is little merit in the ultimate, since in the end political forces, if they are strong enough, can always overcome legal restraints, and a system which will not bend will break. All that I am concerned to point out is that the supposed impossibility of any sort of entrenchment in our existing constitutional system is imaginary.

OTHER DEVICES

I do not see much to be said for some other devices which have been pressed into service in order to give rigidity to constitutions. One is to enact that no amending legislation, unless passed in the prescribed way, shall be presented for royal assent, with the implication that presentation for royal assent contrary to the Act might be prohibited by injunction. This device has had something of a vogue in Australia,[44] and though the propriety of the courts intervening was doubted by the highest possible authority, Sir Owen Dixon C.J., that doubt might have been removed had the draftsman thought of expressly empowering the court to grant the injunction. But perhaps we should accept the conclusion of another high authority, Sir Zelman Cowen, formerly Governor-General, that no conceivable form of drafting can empower the courts to intervene at this stage of the Parliamentary process.[45] If that is right, this device must be rejected. It is in any case a clumsy one, disliked by judges and likely to embroil the courts with Parliament.

The prize for bizarre forms of entrenchment must undoubtedly be awarded to the government of Sri Lanka. In framing the draft constitution for that "Democratic Socialist Republic" in 1978 the government included a clause making advocacy of any constitutional amendment a criminal offence punishable with up to 10 years' imprisonment, with or without fine, and with forfeiture of all property.[46] After enduring this lecture you may think this the best of all the suggestions, since it should effectively silence professors of constitutional law. In Sri Lanka, however, second thoughts prevailed, and ultimately a normal type of amendment clause was adopted, with no criminal penalties for activating it.

So I return to my own suggestion, elementary though it may appear. It is not a mere device or evasion. It meets the case because it goes to the heart of it. It is in the breasts of the judges that the problem lies and it is in their breasts that we must contrive the solution. If we only acknowledge this, much futile speculation can stop.

[44] See (1955) 71 L.Q.R. 336 (Zelman Cowen).

[45] *Ibid.* 342.

[46] *The Times*, August 8, 1978, p. 5.

Chapter 4

ADMINISTRATION

THE REACTION AGAINST MALADMINISTRATION

If there is one word in our language which is more ruthlessly overworked than the rest, it must be "bureaucracy." As a schoolboy I was taught that only the illiterate invented words by mixing the Greek and Latin languages, and what can there be said for a word which mixes Greek with French? Yet it has been with us for a century and a half, having been invented, as one might guess, early in the age of reform, when it suddenly occurred to our ancestors that radical improvements in society might be made by passing Acts of Parliament and appointing officials to administer them. There had been plenty of Acts of Parliament beforehand, but with the reform legislation there arrived something different: discretionary power. This was the hallmark of the administrative age, heralded most notably perhaps by the Poor Law Amendment Act 1834. A new word was needed to describe the new administrative empires which were arising, and "bureaucracy" had the merit of the derogatory flavour which its linguistic illegitimacy helped to convey.

From that time onwards the battle over discretionary power was joined, some saying that it was an abomination which could not be reconciled with the rule of law, others resigning themselves to their fate while continuing to denounce bureaucracy. Some maintained that the constitution supplied an adequate restraining mechanism through the doctrine of ministerial responsibility to Parliament; and so perhaps it did for a time, at least in respect of major decisions of policy on which parliamen-

pinion could be mobilised. But this comforting proposition became less and less tenable as the party system grew in efficiency and in rigidity and as it became obvious that Parliament had become the obedient instrument of the government of the day. But even if Parliament had maintained its independence, it would have been quite incapable of controlling the flood tide of discretionary power which surged forth after the Second World War. Its pressure was reduced by the use of special tribunals to dispose of cases where the decision could be made according to rules, and a large part of the administration of the welfare state could be handled in this way. But the rules themselves were often made at the discretion of ministers and they had large reserves of power under skeleton legislation of the kind which was the basis, for example, of supplementary benefit. Another expedient, and a very important one, was the Parliamentary Commissioner for Administration, alias the Ombudsman, whose place in the system was judiciously assessed by Sir Kenneth Wheare in his Hamlyn Lectures of 1973. After a reluctant start the Parliamentary Commissioner soon learnt to involve himself in the decisions of government departments, and of ministers also, whenever there was a complaint of abuse, unfairness or other maladministration; and although he has no power to lay down the law, he has great persuasive power, so that government departments usually make amends, sometimes by the payment of large sums of money. And his counterparts, the local commissioners, have succeeded similarly. The administrator now knows that the eyes of the ombudsmen are upon him. The decline in the effectiveness of Parliament has at last been compensated—and by a new institution.

It has been compensated in addition by an old institution, the courts of law. In the legal history of the last 30 years there has been nothing more remarkable than the awakening of the courts to the need to remedy abuse and

unfairness in government. In his book *The Discipl[*]
Law* Lord Denning made it clear that the law's greatest
task at the present juncture was to control and remedy
the abuse of power, whether by the government, big
business or powerful trade unions. The role of the courts
will be the subject of my last lecture, but here I may
mention the effect on administration and the healthier
balance of power between the judiciary and the executive
which has been achieved. The judges have been embroiled in a series of battles against the misuse of power at
the highest level and have established, or rather re-
established, some very salutory restraints.

In terms of realities the results are certainly striking.
We could fly to North America more cheaply, thanks to
the decision in the *Laker* case.[1] The *Congreve* case[2]
established that the Home Secretary may not, as he
supposed he might, cancel our television licences if we do
something quite lawful but of which he disapproves. In
the *Tameside* case[3] the Secretary of State for Education
and Science had claimed to be able to dictate policy to a
local authority on the question of comprehensive schools
versus grammar schools, when in fact he was empowered
to intervene only if the local authority were acting
unreasonably. In the *Padfield* case,[4] a few years earlier,
the House of Lords had, as it were, set the scene for
these events by rejecting a minister's claim that a discretionary power under the milk marketing scheme gave
him an unfettered power to decide just as he liked, and
by emphasising in broad terms that unfettered discretion
is something that the law does not admit. If it were
otherwise every one would be helpless in the face of the

[1] *Laker Airways Ltd.* v. *Department of Trade* [1977] Q.B. 643.
[2] *Congreve* v. *Home Office* [1976] Q.B. 629.
[3] *Secretary of State for Education and Science* v. *Tameside Metropolitan Borough Council* [1977] A.C. 1014.
[4] *Padfield* v. *Minister of Agriculture, Fisheries and Food* [1968] A.C. 997.

unqualified powers which ministers find it so easy to obtain from Parliament. So the judges have to this extent been able to give protection against the excesses of the "elective dictatorship" to which I made reference in my previous lecture. It would be wrong to say that they have invented new doctrines for the purpose, and taken more power into their own hands. What they have done is to activate principles which have been embedded in the law for centuries, and to apply them with far greater confidence and vigour than they were willing to do 30 or 40 years ago. There has been little change in the law itself, but a very marked change of judicial spirit. Of that I will have more to say in my next lecture. My purpose now is to look at some aspects of the administrative machine as revealed by these cases and various other events and to point to a few features which call for legal comment.

OVER-STRETCHING OF POWERS

In the first place, it is notable that a number of the cases have concerned the misuse of power by ministers themselves in deliberate decisions of policy. Today I think that no one would make the comment, which used occasionally to be heard, that the courts are more severe with local authorities than with the central government. I do not think that this was ever true, but that is now immaterial. What does seem to be true, and what is perhaps obvious, is that the more power governments enjoy, the more misuse of it there will be. Whatever the reasons, we have witnessed during the last few years this succession of cases in which ministers have been tempted to strain their powers up to and beyond their limits, instead of following the prudent course of keeping a comfortable distance within them. In the *Congreve* case the Wireless Telegraphy Act 1949 provided simply that a television licence "may be revoked or . . . varied" by the Home Secretary and his advisers supposed that because this was, taken literally, an absolute and unqualified power, therefore he could use it to penalise people who took out their television licences a little earlier than usual in order to obtain them before the fee went up. Parliament is far too prone to grant blank cheque powers of this kind and ministers, through their legal representatives, have been too prone to argue that blank cheque powers could be used or abused in any way that suited them. They did not seem to appreciate that this was a kind of constitutional blasphemy. The law has always maintained that powers are to be used reasonably and in accordance with the true purposes of the statute, and in the *Padfield* case the House of Lords emphatically repudiated the whole idea of "unfettered discretion" in the context of the milk marketing scheme.[4a] The Parliamentary Commissioner, who condemned in unsparing terms the Home Office's handling of the television licence business, said that he could not criticise the Home Secretary for acting on the advice of his own lawyers. But one wonders how it could ever have been supposed that licences could properly be revoked merely because their holders had exercised their undoubted legal right to take them out at an earlier date and a cheaper rate. When asked in the House of Commons whether it would not have been better to take the advice of the law officers, the Home Secretary said ruefully that it would have been better to have taken the advice of someone who had given the right advice.[5] But between the lines of the handsome apology which he made to the House of Commons, and in his decision not to appeal to the House of Lords, one may detect his own conclusion that this unhappy affair, as he called it, was a textbook example of abuse of executive power. It had simply not been

[4a] It has done so again in the context of refunding of overpaid rates in *R.* v. *Tower Hamlets L.B.C., ex p. Chetnick Developments Ltd.* [1988] 2 W.L.R. 654.

[5] 902 H.C. Deb. 238 (December 9, 1975).

foreseen that the rise of the licence fee would be anticipated and the B.B.C.'s revenue diminished. The Home Office had attempted to make up for a bureaucratic failure by resorting to a blunt instrument which it had no right to use in such a way.

There was equally obvious abuse in the *Laker Airways* case. The Civil Aviation Act 1971 provided categorically that one of the duties of the Civil Aviation Authority was to allow at least one independent British airline to compete with British Airways. It also allowed the Secretary of State to give mandatory "guidance" to the Authority, but only "with respect to the functions conferred on it." Since one of these functions was to allow independent competition, it should have been obvious that the Secretary of State was acting unlawfully when he gave "guidance" to the Authority which in effect required them to cancel the licence for the Laker Skytrain so that British Airways should have a monopoly. Parliament had expressly enacted that competition by independent airlines was to be allowed and the Act was deliberately used by the government for the purpose of preventing it. Here again one sees a minister, acting no doubt on legal advice, stretching his powers in order to frustrate the express policy of Parliament. This is the disquieting feature of the series of cases which have come close together quite recently and which seem to indicate a tendency to strain statutory powers in the way the Stuart kings strained the royal prerogative.

Even the prerogative may no longer be a source of free discretionary power. It played a prominent part in the *Laker Airways* case, and now is a good occasion for taking stock of it. In addition to their attempt to put the Civil Aviation Act 1971 into reverse by issuing "guidance" under it, the government proposed to cancel Laker's designation under the Bermuda Agreement of 1946, with the result that the United States government denied landing rights to Laker. This was action by the

Crown in the realm of foreign affairs, outside the jurisdiction and beyond the reach of judicial review, as the
Crown contended. But the Court of Appeal, rising to the
occasion, held that the prerogative power of the Crown
had been impliedly restricted by the provision about
competition in the Civil Aviation Act, and that it was an
abuse of the prerogative to use it in a way that frustrated
the express requirement of the Act. So here was another
element of abuse and another attempt to render an Act
of Parliament nugatory by executive action. Lord Denning M.R., going further than the other members of the
Court, said:

> "Seeing that the prerogative is a discretionary power
> to be exercised for the public good, it follows that its
> exercise can be examined by the courts just as any
> other discretionary power which is vested in the
> executive."

He went on to refer to Hampden's challenge to the
prerogative over ship money, and to hold that the court
can examine the exercise of discretionary powers of all
kinds, "to see that they are used properly and not
improperly or mistakenly." If this doctrine should establish itself—and seed scattered by Lord Denning often has
remarkable powers of germination—a new and important
dimension will have been added to the principle of the
Padfield case, that there is no such thing as unfettered
executive discretion. Nor is Lord Denning the only judge
to have suggested that the court's arm might be long
enough to reach into the sphere of prerogative.[6]

---

[6] Lord Devlin said the same in *Chandler* v. *D.P.P.* [1964] A.C. 763,
809–810. The House of Lords has since corroborated the proposition in
Council of Civil Service Unions v. *Minister for the Civil Service* [1985]
A.C. 374.

WHAT IS "PREROGATIVE"?

But what does "prerogative" mean? I have felt disposed
to criticise the use of this term in some recent judgments
and other contexts where, as it seemed to me, no
genuine prerogative power was in question at all. If
prerogative power is to be brought under judicial control, and if ministers are to be condemned for abusing it
unlawfully, it is worth finding out what it really is. In the
first place, the prerogative consists of legal power—that
is to say, the ability to alter people's rights, duties or
status under the laws of this country which the courts of
this country enforce. Thus when Parliament is dissolved
under the prerogative it can no longer validly do business. When a man is made a peer, he may no longer
lawfully vote in a parliamentary election. When a university is incorporated by royal charter, a new legal person
enters the world. All these legal transformations are
effected in terms of rights, duties, disabilities, etc., which
the courts will acknowledge and enforce. The power to
bring them about is vested in the Crown by the common
law, so it clearly falls within the definition of the royal
prerogative as "the common law powers of the Crown."
But when the government cancels the designation of
Laker Airways by making a communication to the government of the United States under the terms of an
international agreement, that has no effect under the law
of this country whatsoever and has nothing to do with
any power conferred by common law or recognised by
British courts. It may be, as the Court of Appeal held, an
act prohibited by a British statute. But it is not an act of
power in any British constitutional sense, since it
involves no special power that a British court will recognise. Whatever powers the government may have had
under the Bermuda Agreement were powers in the
sphere of international law, and their capacity to make
the Agreement came not from common law but from

their status in international law as an international person. In the *Laker Airways* case the Attorney-General claimed that the Crown was entitled to cancel the designation under the royal prerogative, and there was much talk about prerogative in the judgments. But if there was no power, in the correct legal and constitutional sense, there was no prerogative either. There was merely a piece of administrative action on the international plane.

Another example shows another species of inaccuracy. The Criminal Injuries Compensation Board is an instance of the practice, dear to the administrative heart, of doing things informally and extra-legally if means can be devised. This Board pays out several million pounds of public money annually to the victims of violent crime. But until recently it had no statutory authority.[6a] Parliament simply voted the money each year, and the Board dispensed it under the rules of the scheme, which were laid before Parliament by the Home Secretary but had no statutory force. Nevertheless, by a feat no less imaginative than in the *Laker Airways* case, the courts assumed jurisdiction to quash decisions of the Board which did not accord with the rules of the scheme. In doing so, they described the Board as "set up under the prerogative."[7] But one essential of "prerogative," if I may be forgiven for saying so, is that it should be prerogative. Its etymology means that it should be some special power possessed by the Crown over and above the powers of an ordinary person, and by virtue of the Crown's special constitutional position. Blackstone explained that "it must be in its nature singular and eccentrical,"[8] and can comprise only

---

[6a] The Board was made statutory by the Criminal Justice Act 1988.
[7] *R.* v. *Criminal Injuries Compensation Board, ex p. Lain* [1967] 2 Q.B. 864, 881, 883.
[8] Comm. i, 239, citing Finch, *Law*, p. 85.

"those rights and capacities which the King enjoys alone, in contradistinction to others, and not to those which he enjoys in common with any of his subjects; for if once any one prerogative of the Crown could be held in common with the subject, it would cease to be prerogative any longer."

Now if we apply this test to the constitution of the Criminal Injuries Compensation Board, it is surely plain that the government, in establishing it, was merely doing what Miss Hamlyn did when founding this lectureship and what any of us could do if we had the money ready to hand. We could set up a board, or a committee, or trustees with authority to make grants according to whatever rules we might please to lay down. Thousands of foundations or trusts have been set up in the exercise of exactly the same liberty that the government exercised in the case of the criminal injuries scheme. So far as the Crown came into the picture at all, it was exercising its ordinary powers as a natural person, which of course include power to transfer property, make contracts and so on.[8a] Blackstone was quite right, in my opinion, in saying that such powers are not prerogative at all.

Much the same might be said of other powers of the Crown which writers on constitutional law are fond of cataloguing as prerogative, without regard to Blackstone's doctrine. The power to appoint and dismiss ministers, for instance, appears to me to be nothing else than the power which all legal persons have at common law to employ servants or agents, so that it lacks any "singular and eccentrical" element. Ministers as such have no inherent powers at common law and must therefore be counted as ordinary servants.[8b] It is other-

---

[8a] In *R.* v. *Panel on Take-overs and Mergers, ex p. Datafin plc.* [1987] Q.B. 815, 848, Lloyd L.J. expressed his agreement with this argument.
[8b] Contrast *Council of Civil Service Unions* v. *Minister for the Civil Service* (above), where the House of Lords held that civil servants were employed under the prerogative.

wise with judges, who have very great legal powers, and their appointment and dismissal were undoubtedly within the true prerogative before Parliament gave them a statutory basis. I will not go through the whole catalogue of the powers commonly classed as prerogative in text-books and elsewhere, though I suspect that a number of them would not pass the Blackstone test. A collector's piece comes from a hopeless case of 1971. Mr. Clive Jenkins, the trade union leader, sued the Attorney-General in an attempt to stop the government from distributing a free pamphlet on the Common Market at a cost to the taxpayer of £20,000. The judge is reported to have held that the issue of free information is "a preroga-tive power of the Crown" which the court cannot ques-tion.[9] Since all the Crown's subject are at liberty to issue as much free information as they like (and many of them issue much too much of it), I offer you this as a choice example of a non-prerogative.

The truth seems to be that judges have fallen into the habit of describing as "prerogative" any and every sort of government action which is not statutory. It may be, also, that the responsibility for this solecism can be loaded onto that popular scapegoat, Dicey. For his well known definition of prerogative is "the residue of discre-tionary power left at any moment in the hands of the Crown." He makes no distinction between the Crown's natural and regal capacities, indeed at one point he says[10]:

"Every act which the executive government can lawfully do without the authority of an Act of Parliament is done in virtue of this prerogative."

So the judges and authors whose wide statements I have ventured to criticise could quote Dicey against me. But if

---

[9] *Jenkins* v. *Att.-Gen.* [1971] C.L. 1628.
[10] *The Law of the Constitution* (10th ed.), p. 425.

we match Dicey against Blackstone, I think that Blackstone wins. Nor do I think that the criticism is mere pedantry. The true limits of the prerogatives of the Crown are important both in constitutional and in administrative law. This is all the more so now that the courts are showing signs, as in the *Laker Airways* case, of bringing the exercise of the prerogative under judicial control. It may well be easier to extend control to the few genuine prerogative powers which may possibly admit it, for example an improper use of *nolle prosequi*, if the court is not by the same token committed to extend it to all sorts of pretended prerogatives, such as the control of the civil service and the making of contracts or treaties.

PASSPORTS AND THE RIGHT TO TRAVEL

There is another area where the term prerogative is loosely used and where, in addition, an infusion of law is badly needed. This is the matter of passports, or perhaps I should call it the citizen's right to travel. For many years the government has claimed an unfettered discretion to grant, deny or cancel a passport without reasons given or fair procedure or right of appeal or legal remedy, and in the past this supposed power has been used arbitrarily to restrict the rights of British subjects to leave the country and also, it seems to re-enter it. The Immigration Act 1971 made a minor change by providing that a patrial who has the right to leave and enter the realm freely must on proper request show a passport or other satisfactory evidence of his identity and nationality.[11] But he may still be unable to enter other countries without a passport and the denial of it may in practice deny him freedom of travel.

In principle it is highly objectionable that the executive should claim this power of administrative punishment,

---

[11] Sched. 2, para. 4(2)(*a*).

but there is no doubt that it does. A typical statement
comes from the Report of the Committee of Privy
Councillors on the Recruitment of Mercenaries of 1976,
when there was concern over British mercenaries fighting
in countries such as Angola. The Committee said[12]:

> "The issue of a passport is an exercise of the royal
> prerogative and the document, when issued to its
> holder, nevertheless remains the property of the
> Crown. No United Kingdom citizen has a right to
> have a passport issued to him and the Foreign
> Secretary, by whom the prerogative is exercised, can
> withhold or withdraw a passport at his discretion."

They then quoted a parliamentary answer enumerating
the types of person to whom it was the practice to refuse
passports, one of which was "in very rare cases":

> "a person whose past or proposed activities are so
> demonstrably undesirable that the grant or con-
> tinued enjoyment of passport facilities would be
> contrary to the public interest."

This is a polysyllabic way of describing any one whose
activities are disapproved of by the government.

My first comment, which may not now come as a
surprise, is that I question whether passports have anything to do with the royal prerogative in its proper sense.
A passport as such has no status or legal effect at
common law whatever. It is simply an administrative
document. On its face it is an imperious request from the
Foreign Secretary that all whom it may concern shall
allow the bearer to pass freely without let or hindrance
and shall afford him assistance and protection. In reality
it is an international identity card, certifying that a

---

[12] Cmnd. 6569 (1976), para. 18, quoting 881 H.C. Deb. (Written
Answers) 265.

traveller is accepted by this country as one of its nationals. A United Kingdom national's passport does not have the slightest effect upon his legal rights, whatever they may be, to go abroad and return. Those rights are a matter of common and statute law, which the Crown has no power to alter. The Committee on Mercenaries very rightly said that the withholding or withdrawing of passports as a means of preventing United Kingdom citizens from leaving the country could not be justified either pragmatically or morally—and that what effect it might have would be based on bluff, relying on the citizen's ignorance of his right at common law to leave the kingdom and return to it. Since it has no effect on legal rights, the grant or withdrawal of a passport is not an exercise of legal power and cannot therefore represent the exercise of prerogative power. Formerly the Crown did possess the power to prevent a subject from leaving the realm by issuing the writ *ne exeat regno*, which was once a favourite instrument for preventing the clergy from resorting to Rome. That had legal effect, and was therefore a true prerogative power, but it is now held to be obsolete except when granted by the court to a creditor against an absconding debtor. According to Blackstone, if I may invoke him again, "by the common law, every man may go out of the realm for whatever cause he pleaseth, without obtaining the King's leave."[13] Passports do not enter into the legal picture at all.

The important question is whether it is tolerable that the government should wield an unfettered power to deny to a citizen the internationally accepted means of proof of his own identity and nationality. No reasons are given and there is no right to be heard, since the whole matter is administrative and outside the law. In 1968, when the government had taken to withdrawing the

---

[13] Comm. i, 265. See the discussion in *Parsons* v. *Burk* [1971] N.Z.L.R. 244; and an article in *The Times*, August 7, 1968, p. 9.

assports of United Kingdom citizens involved in certain
ways with Zimbabwe, they set up a committee to scru-
tinise and report upon these withdrawals; but it was only
advisory, and only concerned with Zimbabwe. Apart
from that, there is no procedure or appeal of any kind,
not even a right to complain to the Ombudsman.[14] When,
also in 1968, a journalist attempted to travel from
London airport without a passport, as a test case, he was
refused leave to embark.[15] The authorities evidently
knew that he was a United Kingdom national, who
needed no such leave; but they refused to accept his
evidence of nationality and treated him as an alien,
apparently without any good reason. This seems to have
been a plain case of abuse of power, as well as a breach
of the European Convention on Human Rights[16]; but
since no legal proceedings followed the "test case" came
to nothing. The right to leave without a passport is
apparently now recognised. But that by itself is of little
use if the government declines to provide the document
which is required for entry into foreign countries.

This is a murky administrative area where there is a
crying need for clarification and legal right.[16a] It needs to
be recognised, as the American Supreme Court has held,
that freedom to travel is a constitutional liberty closely
related to other basic liberties.[17] It needs to be recog-

Parliamentary Commissioner Act 1967, Sched. 3, paras. 1, 5.
See 765 H.C. Deb., Written Answers, 119 (May 23, 1968).
Articles 2 and 3 of the Fourth Protocol (in force from May 2, 1968)
protect the freedom to leave any country and the freedom to enter
one's own country.
[a] Since this was written the courts have made a breakthrough. In *R.* v.
Secretary of State for Foreign and Commonwealth Affairs ex p. Everett
[1989] 2 W.L.R. 225 both the High Court and the Court of Appeal held
that the refusal of a passport was subject to judicial review and "just as
justiciable as immigration decisions"; but relief was refused in discretion.
Aptheker v. *Secretary of State* 378 U.S. 500, 517 (1964); and similarly
Kent v. *Dulles* 375 U.S. 116 (1958); *Lynd* v. *Rusk* 389 F. 2d 940 (1967).
In India the refusal of a passport at the discretion of the executive is
held to violate the right of personal liberty secured by Art. 21 of the
Constitution: *Satwant Singh* v. *Ramarathnam* A.I.R. 1967 S.C. 1836.

nised, also, that the primary function of a passport is merely to provide evidence of identity and nationality, and that it is as unreasonable to deny this to a citizen as it would be to deny him a copy of his birth certificate. Whether the government approves or disapproves of his activities abroad should have nothing to do with it. As a committee of Justice recommended in 1974, there should be a statutory right to a passport and the courts should deal with disputed cases.[18] Arbitrary power over liberty of movement is really not tolerable, however carefully exercised. As in the other matters which feature in this lecture, there must be some safeguard against abuse. The safeguard against abuse is the law and the courts. The modern type of passport is said to have been introduced by Louis XIV and British practice is still too redolent of his style of government.

OFFICIAL SECRECY

Any investigation of murky administrative areas ought to give a prominent place to official secrecy. But I have two reasons for flitting over it lightly now. First, Sir Norman Anderson surveyed it in illuminating detail in his Hamlyn Lectures two years ago. Secondly, it may be wasted effort to flog a dead, or at least a moribund, horse. It is agreed by all, including governments of both parties, that it is indefensible to keep on the statute book section 2 of the Act of 1911, which makes it a criminal offence to disclose, without authority, how many cups of tea are consumed in a government department. It also seems to be admitted that this absurd law has become self-defeating, since it has lost credibility in the eyes of both judges and juries. It is true that nothing has been done, although in three successive Queen's Speeches two successive governments have promised legislation.

[18] "Going Abroad, A Report on Passports" (1974), *Justice*, paras. 48–50.

Nevertheless it is accepted on all hands that the minimum necessity is an Official Information Act on the lines proposed by Lord Franks' Committee in 1972.[19] The real controversy is whether it is sufficient to make this minimum reform or whether we need a Freedom of Information Act on the lines of the American legislation which has made such an impact in Washington. In the United States "the public's right to know" is championed enthusiastically by Congress, which in 1976 gave to one of the Acts the official short title of the Government in the Sunshine Act. More of this American sunshine would be welcome in what has been called Whitehall's forbidden city. But perhaps this is now only a matter of time. In the White Paper of 1978[20] the former government professed itself willing to go a little further than the Franks recommendations in some respects, while wishing to stop short of them in others. As to a more radical Freedom of Information Act of the American or Swedish type, which would give the public a legal right of access to official documents not covered by specific statutory exceptions, the former government's Green Paper of last year was discouraging.[21] But such an Act had been advocated in the Labour Party election manifesto of 1974; and the White Paper had gone so far as to say that it regarded its own proposals "as a necessary precursor of further change, as well as of improvements of attitudes in the public service."

Still more discouraging, unfortunately, was the abortive Protection of Official Information Bill of 1979, which coincided with the sensation produced by Mr. Andrew

---

[19] Report of the Committee on s.2 of the Official Secrets Act 1911, Cmnd. 5104 (1972).

[20] Cmnd. 7285 (1978).

[21] Cmnd. 7520 (1979). See also *Disclosure of Official Information: A Report on Overseas Practice* (HMSO, 1979), reviewing arrangements in nine other countries. Freedom of information laws were enacted in Canada, Australia and New Zealand in 1982.

Boyle's book, *The Climate of Treason*. The Bill appeared to achieve the remarkable feat of being even more objectionable than the Official Secrets Act. Section 2 of that Act is at least confined to information derived from official sources, whereas the Bill made it a crime for any one to disclose information obtained from any source if it fell within the very wide definitions of protected information, and also was or had been in the government's possession. Had it been law, it seems that Mr. Boyle's book would have been prohibited, even though he obtained his information in the United States under the Freedom of Information Act. Under cover of the furore the government withdrew the Bill, which was under attack on many grounds. So I had to must take back my optimistic remarks. The battle which seemed virtually to have been won was still hanging in the balance.[21a]

It may be worth pointing out, as I ventured to do to the Franks Committee, that the campaign for a civilised Information Act is part of a wider war against official secretiveness, which on other fronts really has been won. It is not so very long since the citadel of secrecy was defended, seemingly impregnably, by four stout bastions: first, the Official Secrets Act; secondly, the concealment of departmental mistakes by an over-rigid doctrine of ministerial responsibility; thirdly, the refusal to disclose inspectors' reports after public inquiries; and fourthly, abuse of so-called "Crown privilege" under which the government used to claim that litigants must be denied access to evidence needed to establish their rights if the evidence fell within the very wide classes which were officially confidential. This last malpractice was brought to an end by a judicial decision of the House of Lords in

---

[21a] Reform was at last effected by the Official Secrets Act 1989, which greatly reduces the impact of the criminal law by restricting the categories of information in respect of which offences can be committed and by requiring the prosecution to show harm to the public interest in certain cases.

1968[22] which was another of the milestones on the road of reform which the courts were opening up at that time. The second bastion, founded on the fallacy that it was constitutionally impossible to go behind the answer of the responsible minister in Parliament, was blown sky-high in 1967 when the Parliamentary Commissioner was given power to go into the department and find out exactly what had gone wrong where. The third bastion, the non-publication of inspectors' reports, was evacuated in 1958 by a strategic governmental retreat after an earlier Franks Committee had rendered it untenable. One bastion only then held out. After Fox's Libel Act of 1792 governments found that they could, after all, survive without prosecuting any one who criticised them, as they had previously believed was essential. In the same way they will find that they can live with a more liberal information law, just as they can live with the Parliamentary Commissioner, the disclosure of inspectors' reports and judicial control of claims to privilege.

GOVERNMENT BY BLACKLIST

In 1978 there was strong complaint about the government's blacklist, an instrument of oppression which combined both constitutional and legal impropriety. The government, like so many of its predecessors, was attempting to enforce wage control, but it was unwilling to seek powers from Parliament. Instead it resorted to a kind of clandestine administrative warfare. If a firm awarded a wage increase which was more than the government approved, the government put the firm on the blacklist, meaning that it would be discriminated against in the exercise of discretionary powers. Government contracts would not be given to it, it would be denied export credits, investment grants, and any other

[22] *Conway* v. *Rimmer* [1968] A.C. 910.

benefit which a minister controlled. For some time there
was a game of hide and seek with the government
refusing to confirm or deny what it was doing. But when
it all came out into the open there were reports of
finance under the Industry Act being refused to a furni-
ture factory and of a threat to make an order against an
insurance company forcing it to reduce its premiums.
The legality of this technique of coercion was not tested
in the courts, though it assuredly would have been had
not the pay policy collapsed. But one firm, which was
threatened with the loss of government contracts, published an opinion given to it by leading counsel, from
which I quote the following sentences[23]:

> "All this is sought to be justified as being a mere
> exercise by the government of the same freedom to
> contract as is enjoyed by an individual. But, while
> an individual can do anything which is not contrary
> to the criminal or civil law, the government is
> subject to the rule of law in a wider sense.
>
> This usurpation of power by the executive is of
> profound constitutional significance. If permitted, it
> will enable the government of the day to enforce its
> party policies under the pretext of the national
> interest without recourse to Parliament."

That is surely fair comment. If the government wishes to
take new powers, it is fundamental to our constitution
that it should seek them from Parliament, and that they
should be conferred by Parliament, if at all, under the
due forms of law, *i.e.* by statute. The powers are then
defined and the courts can protect the citizen in case of
their abuse. To attempt to govern without Parliament by
abuse of miscellaneous powers, in the manner that the
Stuart kings did by abuse of the royal prerogative, is a
complete repudiation of primary constitutional principle.

[23] *The Times*, February 18, 1978.

The Stuart kings at least had the excuse that the legislation they wanted was difficult to obtain, something which
no government can plead under our present party
system.

The blacklist policy appears to have had an ample
content of downright illegality as well as of constitutional
impropriety. But here a distinction must be made. In
placing its contracts as and how it wishes the government
is exercising the ordinary liberty possessed by anyone
(and I hope no one will call it prerogative). The government's duty not to abuse that liberty is constitutional
rather than legal. It is hardy possible to imagine a court
of law giving a remedy for the withholding of contracts
from a firm which would otherwise have received them,
assuming of course that there is no breach of contract or
other illegality. Unconstitutional, yes; illegal, no. But it
is different where the means of coercion is the discrimi-
natory exercise of discretionary power conferred by
statute. Statutory powers must be exercised for the true
purposes of the statute, and Parliament will be assumed
to have intended them to be exercised fairly, reasonably
and in good faith. To refuse export credits under the
Export Guarantees legislation, to refuse benefits under
the Industry Act, to make damaging orders against
insurance companies under the Insurance Act, all for
purposes entirely foreign to those statutes, must
assuredly be illegal as well as unconstitutional. These
would be plain cases of acting on what the courts call
irrelevant considerations. They would contain the element of illegality which was prominent in the case of the
television licences: the use of powers intended for quite
different purposes in order to penalise the citizen for
doing what is entirely lawful. This is a method of
government which all who care for the constitution and
the rule of law ought to unite to condemn.

At one time the Government of the United States used
to attempt to enforce its prices policy by means of

administrative harassment such as anti-trust investigations. But, like the Stuarts, it could at least say that it was unable to get powers from the legislature. An American friend once told me of his experience as a price control officer during the war. When he told his chief that he did not think the law was strong enough the reply was: "Don't worry about that. If they give any trouble we'll put the inspectors on them." That meant that they would have relays of health and safety inspectors condemning their buildings, their elevators, their fire escapes, their wiring, their drains and so on. That would soon teach them a lesson. At the time I thought how much better these matters were ordered in Britain. But now I doubt.

EXTRA-STATUTORY CONCESSIONS

A sort of negative counterpart to the blacklist is the extra-statutory concession. This is an act of administrative mercy, softening the rigour of the law. Extra-statutory concessions play a considerable part in tax administration, so much so that the Inland Revenue publishes a booklet which sets out many of them as a kind of code. For example, cash paid to miners in lieu of their customary allowance of free coal, even if in law taxable income, is by administrative concession not taxed. It may seem churlish to criticise the authorities for such indulgences, but they also represent an attempt to govern without Parliament in a manner which has provoked strong language from the judges. A notable case[24] concerned income from a big property settlement which the Inland Revenue claimed was in strict law taxable several times over. Since this was, in the words of Walton J., "a monstrous injustice," the Inland Revenue

[24] *Vestey* v. *I.R.C.* (No. 2) [1979] Ch. 198 (Walton J.); [1980] A.C. 1148.

proposed by administrative concession to reduce the liability to what they considered reasonable. Humane as their motives were, the learned judge said that, like many judges before him, he was totally unable to understand upon what basis the Inland Revenue were entitled to make these concessions or why, as in the case of the miners' coal money, one section of the community should be favoured but not others. On the final appeal the House of Lords agreed with him and Lord Wilberforce described taxation by administrative discretion as "a radical departure from constitutional principle."

Lord Radcliffe once said in the House of Lords that he had never understood the practice of extra-statutory concessions when the Inland Revenue had access to Parliament in the Finance Bill at least once a year.[25] Lord Upjohn, in a case where an indefensible tax anomaly had been left unamended for 16 years, said[26]:

> "Instead, the Commissioners of Inland Revenue, realising the monstrous result of giving effect to the true construction of the section, have in fact worked out what they consider to be an equitable way of operating it which seems to them to result in a fair system of taxation. I am quite unable to understand upon what principle they can properly do so."

This technique of preserving oppressive legislation but taking a free hand to temper its operation administratively was attacked with spirit by Walton J. as an illegal exercise of the dispensing power, contrary to the Bill of Rights and taking us back to the days of the Star Chamber. To this a pedant like myself may demur. The dispensing power, as exercised by James II and condemned by the Bill of Rights, purported to be a legal power to exempt individuals from the effect of statutes in

[25] *I.R.C.* v. *Frere* [1965] A.C. 402, 429.
[26] *I.R.C.* v. *Bates* [1968] A.C. 483, 516.

a manner which a court of law would recognise. That feature at least is missing from extra-statutory concessions since the Inland Revenue, to do them justice, make no claim to a legal amending power.

A fascinating case came up in 1979 when the Inland Revenue were proposing a "tax amnesty" for a class of printing workers in the newspaper industry who were thought to have had some very high earnings which had escaped taxation. The interesting aspect here was that the legality of the amnesty was challenged by the National Federation of Self-Employed which was given leave by the High Court to apply for a declaratory judgment and an order of mandamus to compel the Inland Revenue to collect the tax. At the time of this lecture the Federation had succeeded before the Court of Appeal in establishing, as a preliminary point, that they had a sufficient interest, *i.e.* locus standi, to proceed with their claim. But an appeal to the House of Lords was pending[26a] in the interesting context that Lord Wilberforce, in his judgment cited above, had said that the Inland Revenue had a legal duty to assess and levy tax upon those liable by law to pay it.

* * *

I have sometimes wondered whether administrative practices of the kind upon which I have ventured to animadvert in this lecture were fostered by the polarity between the legal and administrative mentalities which is so marked in our system of government. In other countries, whether in Europe, North America or Australasia, it seems to be common for entrants to the highest class of

[26a] *R. v. Inland Revenue Commissioners, ex p. National Federation of Self-Employed and Small Businesses Ltd.* [1982] A.C. 617. The House of Lords in effect upheld the Federation's claim to locus standi, though with a variety of opinions, but held that the Federation had failed to show that the Inland Revenue had exceeded their wide powers under the Taxes Management Act 1970.

the civil service to have had some training in law. In Britain it is the exception. Trained lawyers are extremely sparse in our public service, except in the technical capacity of legal advisers. In other words, they have little say in policy-making. On many matters, of which I have given only a few examples, there is a distinct legal point of view, which is perhaps under-represented at the higher levels of the administrative machine where so much discretionary power is exercised. I think, or at least I hope, that officials with legal education and training would understand that, merely because a statute says baldly that the Home Secretary may revoke a television licence, it does not follow that he may do so in order to penalise citizens for acting lawfully; that if a statute says that there shall be competition in civil aviation, it is not right to try to eliminate it by administrative manipulation; that there are deep constitutional and legal objections to government without Parliamentary authority, whether by blacklist or by extra-statutory concession. In the welter of governmental powers public opinion has, I am afraid, allowed too many things of this kind to pass without much protest. It is at least a gain that the Parliamentary Commissioner and the local Commissioners now keep watch and ward to monitor the work of administration and to remedy lapses from the high standards which it normally upholds. The Commissioners and the courts between them have sent a healthy breeze through the administrative tree-tops and I am sure that important lessons will have been learnt.

Chapter 5

ADJUDICATION

Executive Power and Judicial Policy

Many of my 31 predecesors on the Hamlyn rostrum have discussed the work of the judiciary and the challenges which confront them in attempting to adjust the law to the tremendous speed of change in the conditions of life in this century. But none of them has taken as his main theme the position and powers of British judges *vis-à-vis* the powers of the state. Professor Hamson in 1954 made their lamentable position at that time the starting-point for his discussion of the Conseil d'Etat in France, which aroused great interest not unmixed with envy. Lord MacDermott in 1957 devoted part of his lectures on *Protection from Power* to the powers of Parliament and the Executive. Sir Kenneth Wheare in 1973 naturally included the courts in his review of agencies which could remedy maladministration. By that time the judges had recovered much of the confidence which they seemed to have lost when Professor Hamson and Lord MacDermott gave their lectures. In 1974 Lord Scarman made a strong point of the need for a solution of the problems of administrative law, which was, he said, vital to the survival of the rule of law. He was thinking of the social security system and of the need for the legal profession to adapt itself to welfare administration and the world of statutory tribunals, which was the subject of Professor Street's Lectures in 1968. But his words are equally true on the constitutional plane, where the problem is to strike the right balance between efficient government on the one hand and the protection of the citizen against misgovernment on the other. This balance has been sharply redressed in favour of protection of the citizen in the last 25 years or so, and in my previous lecture I mentioned some of the more sensational judicial exploits by which this has been achieved. Since this has been the outstanding feature of judicial policy during this time, I put it in the forefront of my remarks about adjudication.

Today no apology is needed for talking openly about judicial policy. 30 or 40 years ago judges questioned about administrative law were prone to say that their function was merely to give effect to the will of Parliament and that they were not concerned with policy. In reality they are up to their necks in policy, as they have been all through history, and nothing could illustrate this more vividly in our own time than the vicissitudes of administrative law. In the period of their backsliding they declined to apply the principles of natural justice, allowed ministers unfettered discretion where blank-cheque powers were given by statute, declined to control the patent legal errors of tribunals, permitted the free abuse of Crown privilege, and so forth. Then in the 1960s, when the public reaction against administrative injustice had become too strong to be ignored, the judges executed a series of U-turns which put the law back on course and responded to the public mood. The choice of policies before them was wide indeed. One policy was to fold their hands and look no further than the letter of the statute before them. This is what they did in the 'fifties, when in Professor Hamson's words, "provided the forms have been respected the High Court normally declares itself disarmed." The other policy, which they are following now, is to build up a code of rules of administrative fair play which they take for granted as intended by Parliament to apply to all statutory powers, and perhaps even to prerogative powers, and to insist on preserving their jurisdiction even in the face of legislation purporting to exclude it. They had the choice, in other words, between retiring from the field of administrative law and developing it as an effective system. This was a choice between extremes, and entirely a matter for the judges. Many more choices will need to be made, now that the forward policy is in the ascendant. Lord Denning M.R. spoke with refreshing candour in the case where the Court of Appeal, with no precedent before them, awarded damages against a local authority for negligently approving bad foundations laid by a builder: "In the end," he said, "it will be found to be a question of policy, which we, as judges, have to decide."[1]

THE RENAISSANCE OF ADMINISTRATIVE LAW

Looking back across three decades, we can now see that the turning point of judicial policy came in 1963 with the case of *Ridge* v. *Baldwin*.[2] The House of Lords there reasserted, as an essential part of the rules of administrative fair play, the principle that a man is entitled to a fair hearing before being made to suffer under statutory power. So when a local police authority dismissed their chief constable from his office without a fair hearing, the dismissal was held void in law. When Lord MacDermott gave his Hamlyn lectures in 1957 he had to lament the fact that the principles of natural justice did not apply to administrative action. The House of Lords held that this was entirely wrong, one of the great judicial delusions of the post-war years. *Ridge* v. *Baldwin* reverberated round the British Commonwealth where many judges had been perplexed by the unwillingness of our courts, including the Privy Council, to require the observance of natural justice in administrative cases. A torrent of litigation was then generated in which the courts had not only to define the principle but also to work out the details, dealing

---

[1] *Dutton* v. *Bognor Regis U.D.C.* [1972] 1 Q.B. 373, 391.
[2] [1964] A.C. 40.

with the right to know the opposing case, and whether there is a right to legal representation, cross-examination, and so forth. The law is still developing, but the important thing is that the courts once again accept, as they had always done except in their period of amnesia, that part of their duty was to require public authorities to respect certain basic rules of fairness in exercising power over the citizen.

All this was in the sphere of procedure. Another five years were to pass before there began an equally dramatic transformation in the sphere of substance. This was brought about by the decisions concerning abuse of discretionary power which I mentioned briefly in my previous lecture. In the *Padfield* case[3] the House of Lords rejected the whole notion of unfettered executive discretion, dear though it was to the hearts of Crown counsel. The essence of their decision was that all statutory power is given for the proper purposes of the statute and for them only: any action which conflicts with those purposes, or is taken for extraneous reasons, cannot be authorised by the statute. So the Minister of Agriculture and Fisheries could not refuse to refer dairy farmers' complaints to the statutory committee under the milk marketing scheme when the situation was exactly that for which the committee was constituted by the Act. This doctrine was carried a step further in the *Laker Airways* case,[4] where the Court of Appeal held that action conflicting with the purposes of the Act might be not merely unauthorised but prohibited. That meant that action taken by the government outside the Act, under the so-called royal prerogative, was illegal if it was intended to frustrate the policy of competition between airlines enshrined in the Civil Aviation Act. Then in the *Con-*

---

[3] *Padfield* v. *Minister of Agriculture, Fisheries and Food* [1968] A.C. 997.
[4] *Laker Airways Ltd.* v. *Department of Trade* [1977] Q.B. 643.

greve case[5] the Court condemned the revocation of television licences when used as a means of extorting money which licence-holders were under no liability to pay. In the *Tameside* case[6] about comprehensive versus grammar schools, where the political content was greater but the legal issue simpler, the Secretary of State had attempted to dictate policy to the local education authority by invoking what was in effect an emergency power when there was no real emergency but merely a difference of opinion.

I have already commented on these events from the standpoint of administration, noting the unfortunate tendency to strain the wide discretionary powers which it is so easy for governments to obtain from Parliament. From the judicial standpoint, do they represent a straining of the proper powers of the court? Before discussing this I must add one more to the list, the famous *Anisminic* case,[7] which to the outside observer, at any rate if he is literal-minded, might seem to be the ultimate in judicial enterprise. The Act in question there provided that a determination of the Foreign Compensation Commission "shall not be called in question in any court of law." But the Commission's ruling against the Anisminic company's claim was allowed to be challenged successively in all the superior courts, ending in the House of Lords where, as a fitting climax, it was held to be void. There was no doubt about the intention of the Act: the Foreign Compensation Commission has to distribute a fund which is never enough to satisfy all the claims, and the object of making its decisions final was to enable the dividend to be fixed and paid without long legal delays.

---

[5] *Congreve* v. *Home Office* [1976] Q.B. 629.
[6] *Secretary of State for Education and Science* v. *Tameside Metropolitan Borough Council* [1977] A.C. 1014.
[7] *Anisminic Ltd.* v. *Foreign Compensation Commission* [1969] 2 A.C. 147.

Yet the House of Lords, drawing on respectable precedents extending over several centuries, felt entitled to disregard the express ban on litigation in any case where the Commission was acting outside its jurisdiction—as, by sophisticated reasoning, the majority held that they had done. The net result was that they had disobeyed the Act, although nominally they were merely construing it in a peculiar but traditional way. Here again is a remarkable instance of judicial policy on the constitutional level. The judges appreciate, much more than does Parliament, that to exempt any public authority from judicial control is to give it dictatorial power, and that this is so fundamentally objectionable that Parliament cannot really intend it. So they have adopted the policy of confining such provisions to the narrow class of cases where there is error but no usurpation of power or, in technical terms, no excess of jurisdiction. In 1978 the Court of Appeal decided that the House of Lords had now made that class so narrow that it no longer existed.[8] If this paradox is right,[8a] it will mean that clauses excluding the courts will be left with no meaning at all and that the judges will be unable to deny that they are flatly disobeying Parliament. So it is a situation full of constitutional as well as technical interest. All law students are taught that Parliamentary sovereignty is absolute. But it is the judges who have the last word. If they interpret an Act to mean the opposite of what it says, it is their view which represents the law. Parliament may of course retaliate—but of that more in a minute.

[8] In the *Pearlman* case (n. 12, below).
[8a] Lord Diplock held that it was right in *Re Racal Communications Ltd.*, reported as *Re A Company* [1981] A.C. 374, but simultaneously the Privy Council held that it was wrong in *South East Asia Fire Bricks Sdn. Bhd.* v. *Non-Metallic Mineral Products Manufacturing Employees Union* [1981] A.C. 363. The conflict is unresolved, though judicial obiter dicta tend to support Lord Diplock's opinion.

LEGISLATIVE AND JUDICIAL POLICIES IN CONFLICT

There is an ancient saying that it is the part of the good judge to extend his jurisdiction.[9] The striking cases that I have been mentioning have caused some people to raise the question whether the judges have been practising this virtue to excess, even though the decisions follow logically from principles which have been familiar for centuries. It is not only executive power which is open to abuse. Judicial power may be abused, and it is not so long since a cabinet minister in the House of Commons accused a High Court judge of being "trigger-happy."[10] Even if the charge was both unfair and out of order, it shows that judges have been thought, in some quarters at any rate, to be pushing their powers to the limit. But there is a third corner of the eternal triangle: Parliament. There can be abuse of legislative power, not indeed in the legal sense, but in a distinct constitutional sense, for example if Parliament were to legislate to establish one-party government, or a dictatorship, or in some other way were to attack the fundamentals of democracy. But, as I have just observed, to exempt a public authority from the jurisdiction of the courts of law is, to that extent, to grant dictatorial power. It is no exaggeration, therefore, to describe this as an abuse of the power of Parliament, speaking constitutionally. This is the justification, as I see it, for the strong, it might even be said rebellious, stand which the courts have made against allowing Acts of Parliament to create pockets of uncontrollable power in violation of the rule of law. Parliament is unduly addicted to this practice, giving too much weight to temporary convenience and too little to constitutional principle. The law's delay, together with its uncertainty and expense, tempts governments to take

See (1968) 84 L.Q.R. 170.
[9] 873 H.C. Deb. 239 (May 7, 1974).

short cuts by elimination of the courts. But if the courts are prevented from enforcing the law, the remedy becomes worse than the disease. Lord Atkin summed it up with his usual felicity when he said: "Finality is a good thing, but justice is a better."[11]

The same lesson may be learned from the case in the Court of Appeal which I have just been mentioning.[12] A tenant was claiming the benefit of the Leasehold Reform Act 1967, under which, if the value of his house was low enough, he could expropriate his landlord without compensation. I will not digress to consider whether that Act was itself an abuse of power in the constitutional sense, as it would be in several countries with constitutions which safeguard rights of property, and as it may be under the European Convention on Human Rights and Fundamental Freedoms,[13] to which this country is a party.[13a] The point here is that the value of the house had to be assessed by the county court, and that for this purpose Parliament had taken away the normal right of appeal to the High Court on a point of law. The County Courts Act 1959 provided also that county court judgments should be immune from judicial control except by way of appeal, so when Parliament took away the right of appeal in the Leasehold Reform Act all roads to the courts were barred. This was presumably intended to make things easier for tenants when expropriating their landlords. But on the point at issue, which was whether central heating installed by a tenant was in law within the class of improvements which he could deduct from the overall value, different county courts in different districts

[11] *Ras Behari Lal* v. *King-Emperor* (1933) 60 I.A. 354, 361.
[12] *Pearlman* v. *Harrow School* [1979] Q.B. 56.
[13] The First Protocol (Art. 1) provides that "no one shall be deprived of his possessions except in the public interest." The Act allows the tenant to expropriate the freeholder for his private benefit only.
[13a] The European Court of Human Rights has since held that the Act does not violate the Convention: *James* v. *United Kingdom* (February 21, 1986) E.C.H.R. Series A, Vol. 98.

were giving different decisions, and Parliament had cut off the only means of settling the matter decisively. It was the tenant who was anxious to go to the Court of Appeal, where he won his case. But he was only able to do so because the Court refused to obey the statutory veto. This makes a textbook example of the misguided policy of preventing the higher courts from doing what they exist to do.

Direct attacks on the jurisdiction of the courts, as in the original Foreign Compensation Act, are relatively rare. A much commoner phenomenon is the indirect attack, which is made by granting power in such wide and subjective terms that there appears to be nothing left for the court to judge. The technique here is to give power conditioned merely by such phrases as "if the minister is satisfied," "if the minister is of opinion," or "if it appears to the minister." This is a favourite formula with Parliamentary draftsmen in their unwearied attempts to create uncontrollable discretion, the intention being that the minister need only swear an affidavit declaring that he had the necessary satisfaction or other state of mind for the court to be precluded from inquiring whether facts really existed which would justify exercise of the power. For over 40 years the judges have been showing signs of resistance to these insidious provisions and now in the *Tameside* case[14] the House of Lords has confirmed that they are not to be disarmed so easily. The Education Act allowed the Secretary of State to dictate policy to the local education authority "if the Secretary of State is satisfied" that they are acting or proposing to act unreasonably. Mr. Mulley was entirely satisfied in his own mind that the grammar schools should be replaced by comprehensives, so he proceeded to intervene. Both the Court of Appeal and the House of Lords explained to him that he had misunderstood the

---

[14] n. 6, above.

Act. If he was required to be satisfied that certain facts existed, particularly if they involved an imputation of some one's acting discreditably or unreasonably, it was for the court to inquire whether those facts existed and whether the Secretary of State had directed himself properly about them. Since there was merely a difference of policy between him and the local authority, and neither policy could be said to be unreasonable in the legal sense, Mr. Mulley's intervention was unjustified. In such a case, therefore, the courts treat the formula "if the Secretary of State is satisfied that a local education authority is acting unreasonably" as meaning "if in fact a local education authority is acting unreasonably"—or, since it is the same thing, "if the court is satisfied that a local education authority is acting unreasonably." Liberties are taken with the literal meaning of the words which, though not so daring as the liberties taken in cases like *Anisminic*, are just as necessary if the judges are to make any effective resistance to Parliament's attempts to deprive them of their proper function. It is abuse of legislative power, as well as abuse of executive power, against which they are fighting.

ANTAGONISM OR TOLERATION?

Brainwashed though British lawyers are in their professional infancy by the dogma of legislative sovereignty, they ought to excuse rather than criticise the logical contortions and evasions to which judges must resort in their struggle to preserve their powers. I do not see how they can fairly be accused, to borrow words used by Lord Devlin (see below), of moving too far from their base. They would be much more open to criticism if they remained content with the wretchedly narrow base to which they confined themselves 30 years ago, when they took clauses of the "if the minister is satisfied" type at face value. For judicial control, particularly over discretionary power, is a constitutional fundamental. In their self-defensive campaign the judges have almost given us a constitution, establishing a kind of entrenched provision to the effect that even Parliament cannot deprive them of their proper function. They may be discovering a deeper constitutional logic than the crude absolute of statutory omnipotence.

It is high time, as it appears to me, that Parliament itself woke up to these issues and ceased to enact legislation in terms which drive the judges to evasive action. A section removing certain restrictions on judicial review was, indeed, incorporated in the Tribunals and Inquiries Act 1958 (now 1971),[15] on the recommendation of the Franks Committee, and so far as it goes it is beneficial. But there is a need for closer scrutiny of this aspect of legislation, which at present seems to arouse little interest in either House. If subjective conditions and similar devices were not so freely used, there would be less need for the courts to spin the webs of sophisticated reasoning which may entangle ministers. Furthermore, it has become evident that the process is counterproductive. The more governments try to give themselves uncontrollable power, the more the courts frustrate them by extending the categories of review. Since these categories are formulated in general terms, such as acting on irrelevant grounds or for purposes not connected with the statute, the end result is likely to be more judicial control rather than less. An example is the case under the Leasehold Reform Act which I have already instanced. If Parliament had not removed the right of appeal, the Court of Appeal would not have been driven to propound a sweeping doctrine which goes even beyond the high-water mark set by the House of Lords in *Anisminic*, and allows the court to interfere

[15] s.11 (1958); s.14 (1971).

whenever there is any kind of mistake of law, notwithstanding a clause in the Act forbidding it to do so.

Some comments on the *Padfield* and *Tameside* cases were published by Lord Devlin,[16] who raised the question whether in the *Padfield* case the courts might have "moved too far from their base." Their base, he said, was the correction of abuse. He was content with the present approach of the judges in general, but seemed to think that they may have gone too far in *Padfield*. His two punch lines are these: "judicial interference with the executive cannot for long greatly exceed what Whitehall will accept"; and "The British have no more wish to be governed by judges than they have to be judged by administrators." One can see the element of truth in both statements, but they savour more of the 'forties and 'fifties, when the law was at its nadir, than of the 'sixties and 'seventies when it has been recovering. Lord Devlin spoke of possible retaliation by Acts providing that a minister's decision may not be reviewed in any court of law. "And that," he says, "puts the lid on." But the *Anisminic* case showed just the opposite, when the House of Lords removed the lid and threw it away.

And did Whitehall put the judges in their place, in the way Lord Devlin suggests? Again, just the opposite. It is true that at first the government proposed to retaliate with an Act purporting to "put the lid on" and disarm the courts entirely. But legal opinion mobilised against it, pointing out that it was contradictory to lay down the law about foreign compensation but then to prevent the courts from seeing that it was correctly applied. Thereupon, to their credit, Whitehall gracefully yielded and Parliament made provision, within reasonable limits, both for judicial review and for a right of appeal.[17] So instead of being punished for their disobedience to an

16 *The Times*, October 27, 1976, p. 12.
17 Foreign Compensation Act 1969, s.3(2), (10).

Act which had tried to "put the lid on," the judges emerged stronger than before and still on speaking terms with Whitehall. So long as they choose their ground equally prudently, and so long as Whitehall reacts with equal good sense, fears about putting the lid on should prove chimerical.

If we respect what little there is of our own constitution, it ought not to be left to Whitehall to say how much judicial control they will or will not tolerate. It is just as much for the judges to say how much abuse of power they will or will not tolerate. This is the part that the constitution assigns to them and they should be allowed to play it, free from threats and accusations and without talk of government by judges. Perhaps it would be too much to hope that this country should be like Australia where, incredible as it may seem, senior civil servants advocate more judicial review as a stimulus to efficiency and morale.[17a] But I see no reason to suppose that Whitehall will fail to understand the need for a better equilibrium than our lopsided constitution provided only a few years ago. There was, it is true, the somewhat bizarre incident in the *Congreve* case where counsel for the Home Office told the Court of Appeal that if they interfered with the revocation of the TV licences "it would not be long before the powers of the court would be called in question." Lord Denning took this as not said seriously, but "only as a piece of advocate's licence"; and counsel later made an elaborate apology to the court.[18] There seems to be no need to magnify this unusual incident or to treat it as evidence of machiavellian designs in Whitehall. The unjustified revocation of the TV licences was as plain a case of abuse of power as there could be, and if Whitehall would not tolerate that it would tolerate very little judicial review at all.

[17a] See below, p. 92.
[18] *The Times*, December 9, 1975.

Progressive Commonwealth Legislation

That other governments accept the need to strengthen the hand of the judiciary may be seen in reforms recently made overseas. Important studies have been made in Canada and Australia and, what is more, they have been followed by legislation. The scope of judicial review was extended in Canada in 1971 both by the Federal Court Act and by the Judicial Review Procedure Act of Ontario. It has been extended in Australia by the Administrative Decisions (Judicial Review) Act 1977, which together with the Administrative Appeals Tribunal Act 1975 forms part of an important package of legislation for the strengthening of administrative law at Commonwealth level. To a certain extent this legislation corresponds to the reforms made in Britain in 1958 by the Tribunals and Inquiries Act, in 1967 by the Parliamentary Commissioner Act and in 1977 by the rules of court which reformed the procedures for obtaining the various remedies. But to a certain extent also it goes further. It abolishes the traditional but illogical distinction between those errors of law which appear on the face of the record and those which do not, so that the court is no longer prevented from quashing a legally erroneous decision merely because it does not display its error on its face. The Australian Act, furthermore, gives a right to a written statement of findings of fact and reasons for wide classes of administrative acts and decisions not covered by our own Tribunals and Inquiries Act. It also catalogues the various heads of judicial review, confirming a number which might otherwise have been doubtful, such as lack of evidence to justify a decision. It does not fall into the trap that sometimes ensnares codifiers, by failing to provide for future developments. For it leaves an open door for acts and decisions which would be "otherwise contrary to law" or would in any way constitute abuse of power.

The whole tenor of this enlightened Act is to confirm and consolidate the jurisdiction of the courts in all the areas which have now been opened up, without prejudice to the future. In addition, the Administrative Appeals Tribunal Act constitutes an Administrative Review Council charged with the task of monitoring the operation of administrative law in the Commonwealth sphere. This is an advisory body comparable in some ways to the British Council on Tribunals, but with much wider terms of reference. It has to inquire into the adequacy of the law and practice relating to judicial review and recommend improvements. It has also to keep under its scrutiny the classes of administrative decisions which are not subject to review, whether by court or tribunal, and make recommendations if it considers that they should be. It may propose ways and means of improving the procedures for the exercise of administrative discretions. It is concerned with the constitution and procedures of statutory tribunals and similar bodies. It will have a programme of research. All this activity adds up to a superintendence over the whole of federal administrative law. It was a body of just this kind that Lord Scarman in his Hamlyn Lectures advocated for Britain, I hope not in vain.[18a]

It follows, and here again there is a contrast with our own Council on Tribunals, that the membership of the Administrative Review Council is primarily legal. Its members must have extensive experience in public administration or else extensive knowledge of administrative law. The Chairman of the Law Reform Commission is an *ex officio* member. Mr. Justice Brennan, the President of the strong team which began work in 1976, wrote in his foreword to the Council's first report that the

---

[18a] It is advocated also in *Administrative Justice—Some Necessary Reforms*, the report of the JUSTICE—All Souls Committee (chairman, Sir Patrick Neill Q.C.), in which many improvements are recommended.

size of its charter was large and it was hard to overstate
the importance of the issues encompassed by it. "They
concern the balance between the citizen and the government," he wrote, "a balance which is critical to a free
society." When the Council first met the Attorney-
General told it that under the new legislation Australia
would have, at the Federal level, one of the most
advanced systems of administrative law in the world.

ANTIPODEAN AND EUROPEAN COMPARISONS

In case you disbelieve what I said earlier, that in Australia the extension of judicial review is favoured even by
civil servants, let me quote two Australian experts,
authors of a valuable book. They say[19]:

> "During discussions with the Bland Committee
> many senior public servants, including permanent
> heads of departments, expressed no opposition to
> either tribunal or judicial review; they recognised
> the possibilities of error and thought that in these
> times the public should not, and would not, accept
> arbitrary decisions reached by public servants in
> private—especially when those decisions adversely
> affected individual rights and interests. Many
> thought that a system of review would not only serve
> the ends of justice but also that efficiency and
> morale in the public service would be improved . . .
> They also could see major advantages in the idea of
> an administrative court or division because the
> judges would then come to understand more clearly
> the problems faced by administrators. At some high
> level seminars too, we have witnessed a curious
> situation in which professional lawyers and academic
> administrative lawyers urged a restrained approach

[19] Whitmore and Aronson, *Review of Administrative Action*, p.
33.

towards judicial review whilst senior administrative
officers advocated extension of review."

What a utopia for lawyers like myself, who have always
contended that administrative law was the friend and not
the enemy of good administration. There is no reason
whatever to suppose that this means government by
judges. It means government by governments, but within
a framework of rules, the judges being the umpires. If I
may repeat, I know of no reason for thinking that the
attitude of senior officials in this country is different from
that of their opposite numbers in Australia, though
certainly it is tacit rather than explicit.

It is interesting that the Australian officials expressed a
preference for an administrative court or division. New
Zealand led the way in establishing an administrative
division of the High Court by the Judicature Amendment
Act 1968, under which administrative cases, whether on
appeal or on review, were allotted to one division which
could thus deal with them expertly and consistently. In
England at this time some cases went to a single Queen's
Bench judge, others to a Queen's Bench Divisional
Court, others to the Chancery Division, according to the
ancient jurisdictional divisions, even though these had
been swept away by the Judicature Acts a century
earlier. It might have been devised as a system for
producing the minimum of convenience and the maximum of diversity of judicial opinion. But now the judges
have themselves supplied the remedy, by giving effect
under rules of court to the recommendations of the Law
Commission.[20] Applications for judicial review are now
concentrated in the Queen's Bench Divisional Court, so
that for practical purposes we have the equivalent of an
administrative division. This arrangement is, in my opin-

[20] R.S.C., Ord. 53, made by S.I. 1977 No. 1955, based on Law Com.
No. 73, Cmnd. 6407 (1976).

ion, much to be preferred to a special administrative court with a legally distinct jurisdiction, since the definition of the jurisdiction would give rise to endless problems. Any one who has studied the law which in France governs the respective jurisdictions of the civil and the administrative courts will need no further persuasion on that point. In our own country administrative law has always been deeply enmeshed with the general law, and so, as it seems to me, it ought to remain, at any rate so long as the results are satisfactory. We need no longer look enviously across the Channel as Professor Hamson did in 1954. With judicial review in the hands of the regular judges, but funnelled through a specialised division, we have the means of obtaining the best of both worlds. In 1954 there may have been a case for unscrambling the omelette, but in 1980 we have, I trust, said goodbye to all that.

My philosophy is far from that of Dr. Pangloss, however, and a good deal of my life is spent in criticising the existing law. But speaking generally, I think that the work of the judges has now rebuilt administrative law to the point where it can stand comparison with other legal systems and may in some respects claim the advantage. May I vouch to warranty Lord Diplock, speaking in the House of Lords in February 1977[21]:

> "In October last, under what I think was a false trade description bestowed upon me by my noble and learned friend on the Woolsack, I attended a meeting of the heads of the supreme administrative courts of the EEC countries in The Hague. The unanimous opinion of all of us was that the result of the method of reviewing abuse of governmental power on the grounds of a breach of fundamental rights would, on similar facts, have substantially the

[21] 379 H.L. Deb. 993 (February 3, 1977).

identical result in all nine of those countries,
that in two of them there are some doctrines,
relation mainly to legislative acts which have not yet
been embodied in English administrative law."

These exceptional doctrines, Lord Diplock explained,
were the principle of proportionality and the principle of
reasonable expectation. "Proportionality" requires that
penalties should be reasonable, *i.e.* that the punishment
should fit the crime; and it has in fact been applied in
England in the decision that a market stall-holder cannot
be deprived of his licence and his livelihood for a trifling
offence.[22] "Reasonable expectation" requires that a
licence-holder should not suffer loss from incurring
expenditure in the reasonable expectation of renewal of
his licence. But I am far from sure that the doctrine of
reasonableness, which has found many applications to
administrative action recently, would not produce the
same result in the same situation. British judges now
react strongly against any element of unfairness, whether
substantive or procedural.

"POLITICISING THE JUDICIARY"

Whenever there is discussion of any extension of judicial
review the objection is raised that it will bring the judges
into politics. We must, it is said, at all costs avoid a
politicised judiciary. I have never found it easy to give
weight to this argument in its context, which is now usually
that of a Bill of Rights. For as with policy, so with politics.
The judges are already immersed in it, and have no hope
of getting out of it. Books, articles and letters in the
newspapers analyse their education and social back-
grounds, accuse them of political prejudice, call their
neutrality a pretence, and insinuate bias because, in

[22] *R.* v. *Barnsley Metropolitan Borough Council, ex p. Hook* [1976] 1
W.L.R. 1052.

selected instances, plaintiffs with bad cases lose them. The judges in the *Tameside* and *Laker* cases are said to have been motivated not by the need to control arbitrariness but by their aversion to certain political policies.[23] The fact that all this is accompanied by much misrepresentation is neither here nor there. The reality is that the judges are under a barrage of political fire. They are constantly having to decide cases which involve politics as well as law, some of which I have criticised myself—but in none of which would I accuse any one of bias or insincerity. That, again, is neither here nor there. The simple fact is that, like every one else, judges live in a world in which brickbats of all kinds are flying in all directions.

Yet among the judges themselves the fear of politicisation is strong. Lord Denning, not normally to be found among the timorous souls, said in a speech in the House of Lords that if judges were given power to overthrow Acts of Parliament they would become politicised, their appointments would be based on political grounds, and their reputation would suffer accordingly.[24] He added:

> "One has only to see, in the great Constitutions of the United States of America and of India, the conflicts which arise from time to time between the judges and the legislature. I hope we shall not have such conflicts in this country."

This was one of Lord Denning's reasons for opposing the enactment of the European Convention in the form of a British Bill of Rights. In a later debate on the same subject the same anxiety induced Lord Diplock and Lord Morris of Borth-y-Gest to oppose it likewise. But other eminent judges think differently, and in the same debate Lord Hailsham made an effective reply, saying[25]:

---

[23] Griffith, *The Politics of the Judiciary*, p. 211 (now 3rd ed., p. 232).
[24] 369 H.L. Deb. 797 (March 25, 1976).
[25] 396 H.L. Deb. 1382 (November 29, 1978).

"We are seriously asked to believe that something awful is going to happen to us if we follow the example of nearly every country in the world."

Then, instancing some of the more sensational judicial exploits, he said of the opposing judges:

"They are under the curious illusion that the judges are not already in politics. Lord Diplock, as one of the authors of the *Anisminic* decision, practically abolished an Act of Parliament about the Foreign Compensation Commission. What about Gouriet? . . . What about the Laker dispute? How about the Tameside education dispute? What about the decision invalidating Mr. Roy Jenkins' policy on wireless licences? How about the various decisions of this House and the Court of Appeal on the Race Relations Act? And what about their recent decisions on the trade union legislation? . . . If they [the judges] assume jurisdiction they are in politics; if they decline jurisdiction they are in politics. All they can hope to be is impartial. . . ."

This is a graphic and rhetorical version of the point which I made prosaically at the beginning of this lecture, when I stressed the wide range of alternative policies between which judges have to choose. If their primary object was to keep out of politics, they would have had to surrender to the executive in all the cases mentioned by Lord Hailsham and in many others. They would be confined to the literal interpretation of Acts of Parliament purporting to give ministers unfettered discretion, and the development of administrative law would be impossible. The law would be back in the shameful position in which it languished 30 years ago.

And why, to take up Lord Denning's point, should judges be horrified at the prospect of having to judge the constitutionality of Acts of Parliament, if they should be

called upon to do so under a new Bill of Rights or a new
constitutional settlement as advocated by Lord Scarman
and Lord Hailsham? This is a primary function of the
judiciary in any country which has a proper constitution.
By a proper constitution I mean one in which no one
organ has unlimited power and in which there is legal
machinery to prevent violation. The Lords of Appeal,
when they sit in the Privy Council, are very familiar with
this activity in interpreting the constitutions of countries
of the Commonwealth, and I do not think that any one
has complained that it has politicised them. If the abortive Scotland Act 1978 had not been rejected in the
referendum, they would have had to sit in judgment on
the validity of Acts of the Scottish Assembly, quite
probably in situations where different parties were in
power in England and Scotland and political tension was
high. If they could face this with equanimity, they could
equally well face the responsibilities of a constitutional
court as suggested by Lord Scarman. One of the reasons
why there is so much dissatisfaction with the constitution,
and why there is so much discussion of the need for a Bill
of Rights, is that its primary proposition, the sovereignty
of Parliament, assigns a subservient part to the judiciary.
It is like a game without an umpire. Consequently the
judiciary do not make the contribution to public affairs
which in other countries is expected of them and is taken
for granted.

It is understandable that judges may prefer the quiet
life of subordination and non-involvement. But there are
dangers in that which to my mind are graver than those
which they fear as potential constitutional guardians.
They are driven, as we have seen, to devious reasoning
of the *Anisminic* type in order to evade statutory
injustice. They must invent imaginary restrictions and
read them freely into Acts of Parliament if they are to
develop a satisfactory administrative law. Although in
the present period they are doing this successfully, it

involves just the same conflict between judiciary and legislature as Lord Denning wishes to avoid. In fact no judge has done more than he to accept the challenge and to dramatise the issues. Bearing in mind the relapses of the past, and the judicial voltes-face which have been needed to rectify them, one may well feel that we need a constitution which indicates in black and white the part that the judges are expected to play. When their position is left unspecified, and they veer from one extreme of policy to another, they are more likely to be accused of political bias than if they are given a proper constitutional status.

We have already an abundance of politically controversial legislation, and I doubt if any Bill of Rights would produce more attacks on the judges than the legislation on industrial relations has done already. They have been the target for abusive remarks by cabinet ministers in and out of Parliament, and many who might have known better, lawyers particularly, have joined in an unseemly clamour at the slightest opportunity, not hesitating to make charges of judicial partiality. I know that, as we are often reminded, Mr. Churchill did the same in 1911,[26] but as every one of my age remembers, his accusations were not always fair. The extremist critics of the judges do not, I think, allow for the unenviable tasks which they have been given by Parliament. If certain organisations or individuals are given a statutory right to commit torts and other wrongs, which others are not allowed to commit, the judges have to decide where the limits of these immunities lie, often with nothing to guide them but imprecise phrases of elastic meaning, such as "in contemplation and furtherance of a trade dispute." Then, in borderline cases, they have to choose between rival interpretations. It is surely to be expected that immunities from the general law will not be interpreted

[26] 26 H.C. Deb 1022 (May 30, 1911).

in the widest possible sense, but will be kept within bounds, subject always to a fair reading of the Act. Otherwise if I may use Lord Scarman's words, "there will arise a real risk of forces of great power in our society escaping from the rule of law altogether." It is surely right that the judicial instinct should be to minimise that disaster. My purpose now, however, is not to join in the political fray, but to illustrate how deeply the judges are embroiled in it willy nilly. All that they can do is to grow thicker skins, in a sadly deteriorating climate. To expect them to change their spots is neither practicable nor right.

The judges must now be utterly weary of the endless discussion of their supposed prejudices, accompanied as it is by the dreary racket of political axe-grinding. It is made a matter of reproach that they are people of good education, that they are middle class, that they have had success in their profession—nothing is too absurd for those who seem to resent the one real safeguard that our distorted constitution still offers. Under all this buffeting they will, we may be sure, stand firm. And when the buffeting is shown to be in vain it will, we must hope, abate. The critics' chorus would do well to take to heart the terms of the Hamlyn Trust: "to the intent that the Common People of the United Kingdom may realise the privileges which in law and custom they enjoy in comparison with other European Peoples and realising and appreciating such privileges may recognise the responsibilities and obligations attaching to them."

EPILOGUE

It has been my aim in these lectures to invite attention to some very diverse aspects of our constitution: the crude and injurious electoral system; the defective mechanism of legislation, and in particular the supposed impossibility of entrenching fundamental rights; the problems of abuse of power, legislative as well as administrative; and the position of the judiciary under the pressures which the political and administrative system now puts upon them. These miscellaneous subjects have one thing in common: they give cause for concern, and no cause at all for complacency in comparison with other countries. But Miss Hamlyn's good intentions may still be fulfilled if we recognise our obligation to study, criticise and improve our constitution, thereby establishing more securely the liberties and privileges which our traditional system has in the past provided. We must recognise that our ancient constitution, if merely left to develop haphazardly, may get badly out of balance, as many think that it has done already. As a country we are temperamentally averse to radical constitutional changes. But we have been willing to face them for Scotland and Wales and we should be no less willing to do so for our country as a whole. People of all political views will need to contribute to the consensus which will be needed. If we could find it, we could become a better governed country and our institutions would better deserve the admiration which Miss Hamlyn had for them.

INDEX

Index

INDEX OF NAMES